Kingsbury.

CW01460660

The World of Indian Miniatures

The World of
Indian Miniatures

❦

JAMILA BRIJBHUSHAN

KODANSHA INTERNATIONAL LTD.
Tokyo, New York & San Francisco

ACKNOWLEDGMENT: all the miniatures are reproduced courtesy of the National Museum, New Delhi.

Distributed in the United States by Kodansha International/ USA, Ltd., through Harper & Row, Publishers, Inc., 10 East 53rd Street, New York, New York 10022; in Canada by Fitzhenry & Whiteside Limited, 150 Lesmill Road, Don Mills, Ontario; in Mexico and Central America by HARLA S.A. de C.V., Apartado 30–546, Mexico 4, D.F.; in South America by Harper & Row, International Department; in the United Kingdom by Phaidon Press Ltd., Littlegate House, St. Ebbe's Street, Oxford OXI ISQ; in Continental Europe by Boxerbooks Inc., Limmatstrasse 111, 8031 Zurich; in Australia and New Zealand by Book Wise (Australia) Pty. Ltd., 104–8 Sussex Street, Sydney 2000; in the Far East by Toppan Company (S) Pte. Ltd., Box 22, Jurong Town Post Office, Jurong, Singapore 22.

Published by Kodansha International Ltd., 2–12–21 Otowa, Bunkyo-ku, Tokyo 112 and Kodansha International/USA, Ltd., 10 East 53rd Street, New York, New York 10022 and 44 Montgomery Street, San Francisco, California 94104. Copyright © 1979 by Kodansha International Ltd. All rights reserved. Printed in Japan.

ISBN 0–87011–340–2
LCC 78–19243
JBC 1071–786760–2361

First edition, 1979

To Brij

for opening unknown vistas before my eyes

Contents

Preface

This is a book intended for the non-specialist. If experts had their way it would never have been written. Whenever I mentioned the idea of this work, it was met with a mixture of scepticism and scorn. Comments ranged from "It can't be done," to "Who needs a book like this? Anyone who wants to find out how to distinguish between various schools of Indian miniature paintings will find out somehow." All this was not exactly encouraging and so the work was shelved for years on end. But I must admit that the longer I live, the more I realize the great need for a sort of ready reference to Indian miniatures.

The number of books that have been written and continue to be written on the subject would comfortably fill many shelves in a library. They seem to fall into three categories—catalogues of pictures with a descriptive text and a general introduction; monographs on particular schools or themes; and general books in which the text carries very little information and the pictures take pride of place. Even catalogues and captions in certain museums are wrong and misleading, and seem to have been done by persons with scant knowledge of the subject. None of these, obviously, are of help to the lay person seeking the basic knowledge of the distinguishing features of the different schools, techniques and subject matter of Indian painting.

Indian and foreign museums are full of Indian miniatures, and there is nothing to guide a visitor and tell him what he is looking at. He reads a caption which says, "Radha and Krishna, Kangra 1800." The foreigner has no idea who Radha and

Krishna are and what Kangra connotes. The Indian, of course, recognizes Radha and Krishna but has no way of judging whether the provenance of the miniature is really Kangra and the date 1800. Why not Garhwal, Delhi, Chamba or Jaipur, and why not 1700? Anyone who has wandered helplessly through miles of tiny pictures with concepts of perspective quite alien to the modern eye will know exactly what I mean. For those who have started their own collection of miniatures on the basis of a sure eye, or after wading through huge volumes not always easily available, the need for a concise comprehensive book on the subject has long been evident. The book is now finally before the public and I hope it will be charitably received.

I have attempted to deal with all the most important schools of painting and the ones that are most commonly met with. Unfortunately, it has not been possible to use illustrations to highlight every point, but most of the books mentioned in the bibliography are full of pictures and they will, I hope, help to clarify various points.

Thanks are due to Mr. O. P. Sharma, Deputy Keeper of the Paintings Department in the National Museum, New Delhi, and to the Museum authorities for making available the pictures for photographing and for permission to publish them. Thanks are also due to Miss Averil Turner for help with the original manuscripts and to Junno and Julie for making a thorny path smooth. Last but not least I wish to thank Mr. Ashim Bose for help with the map and for always being forthcoming with valuable suggestions.

JAMILA BRIJBHUSHAN

New Delhi,
1978

Introduction

Wall paintings and miniatures form the two main categories of Indian painting. Both of these are, by their very nature, perishable, being a natural prey to humidity, heat, insects and a host of other ills including human neglect. The vicissitudes of Indian history, the changing of aesthetic norms and a general apathy toward the need to preserve anything old have all exacted their toll, thus leaving very few extant examples of paintings done in ancient India, between the eighth century B.C. and the ninth century A.D.

The paintings that have survived are all in caves, the walls and ceilings of a great many of which were lovingly covered with finely executed paintings depicting the doings of gods and men. The most famous of these cave paintings are in Ajanta and Bagh (first to sixth centuries A.D.). The caves offered natural protection to the works of art in their depths and helped preserve them reasonably well without the constant restoration that is so much a part of mural paintings in the Western world.

Paintings done on cloth or canvas, which are mentioned in the fourth- and fifth-century plays, *Swapanavasavadatta* and *Abhijana Shakuntalam*, also failed to survive for the above-mentioned reasons. The earliest extant examples of paintings date from the eleventh century and were done on strips of palm leaf about three inches wide and up to a foot in length. They were meant as illustrations for books and certain "pages" contained both text and illustrations. Holes were punched into each leaf and the leaves were bound together with tape or string. The book was then enclosed between wooden covers that were often polished and painted.

These early miniatures received the same kind of protection as the frescoes. Since they were mostly illustrations for religious works of the Jain sect, they were placed within temples and were carefully looked after and preserved.

Gradually, paper replaced the palm leaf as a painting medium, and by the end of the fifteenth century it was in use all over the country, with the exception of certain areas like Orissa, where palm leaf remained popular for another four centuries. The format dictated by the palm leaf, however, remained, and length continued to be more important than height in some schools even after the Persian influence became dominant at the end of the sixteenth century.

The advent of the Middle Eastern invaders after the thirteenth century had a distinct influence on Indian art. Persian painters from Shiraz and Isfahan brought their own forms and techniques, and Indian apprentices working with them or under them blended these with the existing Jain technique. This resulted in rather surprising works where the angular Jain figure existed happily side by side with its smooth, well-formed Persian counterpart.

This style continued in many painting centers in India before the coming of the Mughals, who were responsible for miniature painting as we know it today. This dates from 1555, with the return to India of the second Mughal emperor, Humayun (1507–56), after a long period of exile, one year of which was spent at the court of Shah Tahmasp I (1514–76) of Persia. Much impressed by the high development of the arts and crafts in Persia at this period, Humayun brought back master painters and craftsmen and set them up in workshops in his palace. The fact that these masters could start working immediately with Indian apprentices is evidence of the flourishing state of painting in India at that time.

The earliest products of these ateliers were almost purely Persian in character. As the Indian artist became more at home in the new medium, however, he put his own elements into the work and gradually, from a mere Indian touch in the form of an elephant or human figure, the miniature became more Indian and less Persian.

The Mughal emperors were themselves great connoisseurs of art, and under their patronage miniature painting flourished, resulting in an art form that spread to every part of India, taking on the local characteristics of the area.

As Rai Kishandas, the noted art historian and authority on miniature painting, writes, "The Mughal school of painting forms, as it were, the spinal column of the various schools of Indian miniature art. If the Mughal school had not come into being, the Pahari and Rajasthan schools would not have emerged in the forms in which we find them."

The Mughal court, even after it had lost its power and brilliance, continued to yield a social and cultural influence that can be likened to that of the court of France under Louis XIV. Not only did friends and vassals emulate the dress, etiquette and art forms prevalent there, but enemies also copied the same pattern. Thus, until the rapid changes of the late nineteenth and twentieth centuries transformed the whole social outlook of the country, the Mughal influence was all-pervasive in sophisticated circles, not only in the arts but also in fashion and other aspects of life.

All this is dealt with in detail later, but it is useful here to mention briefly a few characteristics of miniature paintings that will also help in ascertaining their age and provenance.

One characteristic of the Indian miniature is the outline within which every figure is enclosed. This can either be thick or thin, depending on the area and the period from which the painting originates and on the degree of prominence the artist desired to give the figure. But period or region notwithstanding, the confining line is always present. This was only changed when European influences became predominant after the Battle of Plassey in 1757, and the Indian artist was liberated enough to throw off the discipline of centuries and try a new technique.

Since a great many of the miniatures, certainly of the Mughal school, were true mirrors of life in those times, some knowledge of the dress and architecture of the periods is helpful in ascertaining exactly when the work was executed. For example, the four- or six-pointed *jama* (long coat) belongs necessarily to the early part of Akbar's reign (r. 1556–1605), since the fashion was discontinued when it was declared outmoded by the emperor and replaced by the full skirt. Except for some local schools, like the Mewar, which clung to the fashion after it had disappeared elsewhere, pictures showing this mode of dress belong necessarily to an earlier period.

No picture showing Jahangir (r. 1605–27) wearing earrings can ever be dated before 1614, the year the emperor had his ears pierced. Similarly in architecture, the cusped arch, which became popular in the Shah Jahan period (r. 1628–58) only features in paintings done in his time or later. No matter what tale is narrated in the miniature, the scenes are always taken from the everyday life of the area. The subjects are the common people, but slightly idealized—they are never too fat or too thin or have deformities, unless the subject calls for them. The setting is the Indian village, although with none of the squalor generally found in such surroundings.

Although pictures of elephants abound in all schools, thus making it difficult to distinguish one school from another, especially since the drawing of the animal itself is similar in all schools, it is the background, the general atmosphere and the clothes of the mahout that will give us an idea of the provenance. For instance, a red sky, swirling eddies of water, green mounds separating one plane from another and a rock formation would leave little doubt that the picture was painted at Bundi.

Usually a good test of the age of the picture is the fineness of the brushstroke, the painstaking detail of the design and the startlingly vital quality of the picture. Seen under a magnifying glass, all miniature paintings at the peak of their development come amazingly to life. Brushstrokes and expressions not visible to the naked eye are revealed, imparting distinct characteristics and personalities to both humans and animals. No surface is ever solidly filled in. Skin and fur are made up of thousands of tiny brushstrokes, and each hair of the eyebrows and whiskers is skillfully detailed. Each layer of clothing is visible through the outer garments, as are the flesh tone and bone structure of the subject. Works done in the latter part of the nineteenth century show less of this painstaking attention to detail, and strokes are more solid, lines heavier and colors less refined. Colors become much stronger and are laid on with a heavier hand, providing a marked contrast to the delicate molding of earlier years. The tiny strokes which imparted a lifelike quality to skin and hair and transparency to clothes are now replaced by filled-in surfaces which give a more solid and, often, static appearance to the whole. The quality of the color, whether in its softness or its luminosity, could somehow never be recaptured even by the most skillful of the later copyists.

The fineness of the brushwork and the subtlety of color is, therefore, a convenient rule for ascertaining the age of the miniature of the Mughal period or later. The important exceptions are miniatures from Mewar and Basohli which, even at the height of their development, show a distinct folk element and a close adherence to the original Jain school of painting. The colors used are always primary, the drawing simple and uncluttered. Later works show a degeneration in the choice of more effete themes and a closer adherence to Mughal technique.

The differences of each school are given in the succeeding chapters. However, it is well to remember that the best pictures of any school are characterized by vitality, skill of execution and aesthetic composition. This is true not only of the highly sophisticated court art but also of the large number of folk paintings made for the common man all over the country. The older of these have a vitality and an exuberance that is entirely missing in later copies.

The Mughals and some of the Rajput, Deccan and Pahari schools preserved their original drawings in folios. The sketches were often perforated and used as stencils for succeeding generations to copy. Many rulers ordered copies of earlier masterpieces, even to the extent of having the seals of their predecessors affixed on these works. This, however, must be regarded only as what it was meant to be—homage to a great master—and not as an attempt at faking. It can be considered as a copy only in so far as the basic sketch is the same. A study of the technique and the quality of the brushstrokes will immediately reveal that it is not of the apparent period.

One fact to keep firmly in mind is that until recently there have been no clearcut distinctions in India between the arts and crafts. Every craftsman is an artist in his own field, while those commonly considered as artists, such as painters and sculptors, have never striven after distinction by seeking recognition for their creations on an individual level. Art was regarded as the corporate product of a society aimed at achieving harmony, and the artist merely fulfilled his role by helping to create such harmony. An artist, if he was outstanding, was loaded with gifts and honors. No attempt, however, was made to perpetuate his name by inscribing it on his works, which were considered sufficient testimony to his skill and withstood the test of time on their own merit, rather than as the work of an outstanding artist. Nowhere in India, therefore, does one find the equivalent of a Michelangelo or Leonardo da Vinci. The Mughals started by having pictures signed but very soon gave up the practice, thus bringing the art of their period in line with earlier norms.

Indians refer to the various styles developed in the different regions as *kalam*, which literally means "pen" but here it denotes school. Thus, we have the Delhi

Kalam, Kangra Kalam, Deccan Kalam and so on. This does not necessarily mean that the piece was painted in the place its name suggests but that the work is in the style associated with that particular school of painting.

The tremendous revival of interest in the art of miniature painting today has led to the setting up of schools of painting all over India. The paintings produced in these centers imitate old themes and old techniques. In an effort to reproduce the earlier quality of colors, the Indian painter today is experimenting with the natural colors used by his predecessor and trying to avoid the commercial dyes that were responsible for much of the harshness of color in the last century. No matter how hard he tries to capture the technique, however, his work will remain of a lesser quality than the best of the earlier periods. This is partly due to the fact that the miniature painting has hardly any relevance to the mechanized society in India today. Nevertheless, this fact should not detract from the quality of a miniature if it is accepted as a recent work and not compared with earlier works. Miniature painting today should be treated as a strictly twentieth-century product and, therefore, judged on its own merit. The amazing fact about it is its excellence and how closely it does approximate to earlier works. What stops it from being great is the fact that miniature painting is no longer a reflection of the needs and emotions of society but only an attempt to recapture what has gone before.

1

The Traditions

To a people as highly cultured and urbanized as the ancient Indians, the development of the arts was as natural as breathing. The arts of building, especially temples, and sculpting reached such heights of sophistication that their remains even leave the technologically advanced, twentieth-century observers agape with admiration. That painting, apart from murals, of which some are found in 'these temples, had also been lovingly cultivated and extensively practiced is beyond doubt. Ancient plays make numerous references to portraits of the beloved being shown to the lover, accompanied by rapturous remarks about the beauty of the subject and the remarkable way the artist has managed to catch the likeness. Old texts not only mentioned the painter and his work but also laid down meticulous rules about materials and techniques, with detailed tenets as to what distinguishes a good painting from a mediocre or even a bad one.

The making of the preliminary sketch, the filling in of color, the adding in of detail are all described in these texts. The final touch, known as the "putting in of life," was made with the painting of the eyes. This seemingly small detail became imbued with an almost mystic symbolism, for on it depended the vitality of the whole work and distinguished the work of the master from that of his pupil.

The depiction of all categories of people was to be done according to fixed formulae. Thus the *Vishnudharmottara Purana*, an ancient treatise on the arts written in the second century A.D., lays down that holy men be made to look lustrous but emaciated, with matted hair, and that they be clothed in the skin of black deer. Brahmins, or priests, were to be portrayed full of the splendor of their celibate state, clad in white. Ministers of state were to be shown in their full regalia of office, while respectable citizens sported silvery hair, clean clothes and had a courteous and good-natured appearance. The commander in chief, of course, was always to look very proud, with a broad chest and a huge head. He was to be depicted tall and brawny, with a prominent nose and chin and three distinct wrinkles on his forehead. He was always to be shown looking up—whether seeking inspiration or as a sign of hope that his side would win the battle is not stated.

There were also rules laid down for the depiction of each profession. Prostitutes were to be shown heavily made up and gaudily dressed; gamblers, with a bare torso, joyful if winning and sorrowful if losing; workmen were always to be shown engaged in their work; widows gray-haired, simply dressed and devoid of makeup; married women were elegantly dressed, and moderately made up, and when depicted with their husbands, were painted proportionately smaller. Gods were to be represented with hair only on their eyebrows and eyelashes and the rest of their body hairless. Any deviation from the specified size of their halo would lead to the artist's and the patron's ruin and destruction. Even when invoked by a host of Brahmins, the gods were said never to enter an image that was lacking in any of the prescribed touches. A badly executed picture would thus be an invitation to demons rather than to the gods.

Everything was categorized, even the kind of hair and the shape of the eyes of the subject. Hair can be either long and fine, curling to the right, wavy, straight and abundant, curled and abundant, etc., while eyes are said to be shaped like a bow, a fish or a lotus petal.

The postures in which a human figure could be depicted are described in detail along with the specific movement of the limbs. For instance, a person carrying a spear, javelin, pike or other such instrument must walk with the right leg advanced. To indicate fertility, a female figure is broad of hip and thigh, and will have one foot serenely advanced.

The hierarchical concept of Indian society made it compulsory to depict people not only with their trappings of office but also with different colored skins. Certain tribes, people of lower castes, those oppressed by fate and perpetrators of evil deeds were dark-complexioned, while the higher castes and people of standing were invariably given lighter skins.

According to the *Bharata Natya Shastra*, a treatise on drama of the second century A.D., each emotion had also to be given an expressive color. Thus the *sringara rasa* (erotic) was depicted by a darkish hue, the *hasya rasa* (mocking mood) by white, the *karuna rasa* (pathetic) by gray, the *rudra rasa* (furious) by red, the *vira rasa* (heroic) by yellowish white, the *bhayankar* (fearful) by black, the supernatural and amazing by yellow, and the loathsome and repulsive by the same color.

Feelings of love were divided into two main categories: the unhappiness caused by separation (*vihara*) and the happiness of union (*samyoga*). The former could be induced by a host of factors, such as a misunderstanding between lovers or a separation due to a long journey or death. The emotions of united lovers are classified according to external indications, such as a man offering gifts as a token of his love, or a maiden so flustered by the approach of her lover that she wears her ornaments in the wrong places. Evocations of the amorous mood are classified into various forms of coquetry, which include alluring body movements, intensity of gaze and a flurried mien. Other external aids recommended for such scenes are music, flowers, use of red and yellow, humming bees, moonlight.

The colors mentioned in the old texts are gold, silver, copper, mica, tin, iron oxide, deep-colored brass, yellow myrobalan, lac, vermilion and indigo. It is noted that a painting, which is drawn on a canvas that is dipped in the juice of the best *dhruva* grass, does not deteriorate and remains intact for years. Even though the rules for mixing colors are meticulously laid down, the *Vishnudharmottara Purana* concedes the right of the artist to exercise his ingenuity in this field.

The weakness of the drawing and the improper juxtaposition of colors are considered the primary defects of a painting. Shading, too, is specially stressed. A picture devoid of shading is considered mediocre, while one in which some parts are shaded and others left untouched is particularly poor. Recommended methods of producing the effect of light and shade are by crossed lines, stumping and dots.

A good painting is one that is done in golden colors, with well-articulated soft lines, well-arranged garments and well-balanced proportions. Spaciousness of background, its similarity to nature, the variety of themes and the minuteness of execution are all signs of a good picture. A well-produced painting is said to

The Traditions

cleanse the soul, curb anxiety, augment future good, cause delight, kill the evil of bad dreams and please the household deity. It fills the empty places in a house.

According to the treatise on the arts a great artist is one who paints waves, flames, smoke and streamers according to the direction of the wind. He represents the dead as being devoid of any life and the living full of it. Various rules are laid down for landscape painting, especially those depicting the seasons.

Thus, summer is to be associated with a deep pool, with deer under the shade of trees, buffaloes wallowing in mud and human figures in languid poses. The bareness of the landscape, the frenzy of an elephant rushing against rocks and the blissful animal almost totally submerged in water are means by which the artist can depict a burning hot day.

The rainy season is depicted by clouds, lightning, birds in the trees, and lions and tigers sheltered in their caves. In autumn the trees are heavily laden with fruit, the fields full of ripening crops and ponds full of lotus and geese. In winter the sky is covered with heavy fog and men are shown shivering.

General rules for depicting nature are that mountains should be covered with rocks, peaks, trees, waterfalls and snakes; the night sky should be full of stars; the forest should have a thick growth of trees and be full of birds and beasts; water should abound with fishes, tortoises, lotuses. In painting, nature is said to be best represented in its own colors, as if reflected in a mirror.

Since painting, along with other arts, was inextricably linked to religion, the painter was enjoined to dedicate himself to his work in such a way that it became an offering to the deity. He had to sit facing east in a posture of worship before starting on his work. He was expected to study birds, animals and human beings in all their different moods and to meditate deeply on the subject in hand before attempting any major work.

The ancient Indians also insisted that a knowledge of dancing was necessary for a good painter. The *Vishnudharmottara Purana* states, "without a knowledge of the art of dancing, the rules of painting are very difficult to understand." It also says, "Please speak to me about the art of dancing and the rules of painting. You will tell me (afterwards), for (O) Twice-born, one of the rules of dancing implies (those of) the art of painting." Just as a dancer expresses emotion through his poses, so images are given life through the symbolism of gesticulation and pose. Drama, dance and painting must share certain fundamental laws to enable them to become a vital means of communication between the artist and his audience.

Another art with which painting is affiliated is poetry. Like poetry, where suggestion rather than statement forms the basis of expression, so in painting the emotions are to be depicted by the conditions that give rise to them. This means that an emotion should be expressed by the circumstances that provoke it and the outward manifestations of the emotional mood. To take a concrete example, night is depicted by a thief walking stealthily, or a girl going to meet her lover, or a sky full of stars, or the full, half or new moon. A highway is depicted by a caravan, whose size, quality of goods carried and other such details would give an indication of the importance of the highway and the centers connected by it. A battlefield is shown by depicting the four divisions of the army—the cavalry, infantry, elephant corps and chariot corps—and soldiers fighting in a field strewn with bloodied corpses.

The mental and physical state of the artist is equally important since it is bound to be reflected in his work. He must, therefore, at all times cultivate physical and mental fitness and be totally alert, for absentmindedness is said to be one of the main factors responsible for a mediocre work of art.

The painter did not work mechanically. On the contrary, he was totally involved in what he did and took as much delight in the pursuit of his art as others did in looking at it. Old writings describe him as being fully conscious of doing a good job and capable of admiring a painting which is still in the process of being completed. He is described as nodding his head in joyous approbation of the product of his skill.

Artists, whose work took them into palatial homes and magnificent palaces, were nevertheless people of low origin, who mixed only with their own class and did not have access to society. However, their dedication and skill were not only admired and lavishly rewarded, but were the object of much envy. One Buddhist text states that a king watching an ivory carver at work longed to be the creator of the wonderful form that emerged from the artist's hands. Great masters especially were honored with gifts of money and land, and were invited to be judges of works of art.

In the *Kamasutra*, the famous treatise on love, compiled in the early centuries of the Christian era, painting is described as one of the many arts to be cultivated by the *nagaraka*, or gentleman of taste. His room would have a painting board, a casket full of brushes and a beautifully illustrated manuscript, along with a musical instrument and a garland of flowers.

Large cities possessed public and private picture galleries, or *chitrasalas*, and the famous port of the Chola dynasty of the ninth to thirteenth centuries A.D., Puhar, is described as being "resplendent with picture galleries."

For easy accessibility to visitors, the public *chitrasala* had to be located at the junction of four roads, in front of a temple or royal palace or in the center of the king's highway. Provision for adequate lighting was made with many windows, mirrors and chandeliers.

Since looking at an auspicious object on waking up was considered a good omen, those who could afford it had their apartments, including the bedrooms, filled with pictures. Courtesans had elaborate *chitrasalas* which provided the setting for their activities.

Rules were also laid down about the themes of the paintings hung in various places. Themes of love, fun, laughter and peace could decorate private homes and private apartments within the palace. Kamadeva, the god of love, performed his feats in the bedroom, although he also made his appearance in other places. Temples, dance chambers and public places could show any themes that were considered auspicious. In the public *chitrasalas* the themes of the paintings were taken from the epics and from contemporary drama. The more heroic scenes were shown in larger halls and the more intimate in smaller ones. The halls were perfumed, and provided a pleasant place for an evening's dalliance.

Murals were the most popular form of painting and were known as *bhittichitra*, from *bhitti* "wall" and *chitra* "picture." Painting was also done on *pata*, or cloth, which could either be rolled up for storage or stretched over a board and hung.

The fact that none of the latter have survived can, perhaps, be attributed to the vagaries of the climate and the vicissitudes of Indian history. These could only be withstood by the sturdiest of materials, so the only extant artifacts from the workshops of the great universities of Nalanda, Vikramasila, Odantipur, Somarupa and Taxila are stone sculptures, which have weathered the whims of man and nature and have survived as mute evidence of the skill of artists and craftsmen of earlier centuries.

The precepts laid down in the ancient treatises have always provided guidance to the Indian painter. Jain miniatures, the earliest of which date from around the eleventh century, and Rajput and Pahari ones, which date from quite a few centuries later, have obviously been painted with these early instructions in mind. Except for a short break, therefore, during the period known as the Imperial Mughal school, the artist has valued the prescriptions laid down by his ancestors and tried to follow them in the context of his times. The whole range of Indian miniature painting is an amalgam of the natural and the metaphysical. Along with paintings that are based on observations of human beings and nature and are depicted to scale are found others where the human figures completely dwarf their surroundings or a god-man towers above his fellow beings. So skillfully, however, is the perspective handled that the discrepancy never appears incongruous or the result clumsy.

❧ 2 ❧

Materials and Techniques

Paper and Brushes

As noted already, the earliest known miniature paintings found in India are those on palm leaf, which were used as illustrations for Jain scriptures and date from around the eleventh century. Paper came into use in the early fourteenth century, and by the sixteenth century was being extensively produced in India, every quality identified by its place of manufacture. Thus, Daulatabadi came from Daulatabad and Nizamshahi from Nizamabad. It was also classified according to the material from which it was made, e.g., *sanni* (from flax), *mahajal* (from old fishing nets) and *nukhayyar* (watered paper). Other materials from which paper was made were bamboo, jute and waste silk cocoons.

To make for smoothness, the paper was burnished by being dipped in a solution of alum and allowed to become partly dry, after which it was rubbed with an agate or touchstone burnisher. Two or more layers of paper were pasted together to provide the required thickness for painting.

An iron bow pen, with pointed brushlike projections on both sides, was used for drawing straight lines on borders and for making geometric patterns. Circles were drawn with the help of a compass, while a flat ruler was used for drawing lines on borders.

The *Manasollas*, a medieval text, lays down rules for the making of painters' pens. To the tip of a small bamboo style was attached a small nail with only the tip protruding, the rest being embedded in the handle. This was probably used for outlining designs on palm leaf.

Pencils used for drawing preliminary sketches were made from a mixture of cow dung, old powdered slag and water, pounded to a thick paste in a stone mill. When the right consistency was reached it was modeled into pencils of two to four inches in length. The color was light and mistakes could be erased by wiping with a piece of clean cloth. Other sorts of pencils were made of a mixture of lampblack and boiled rice.

Brushes came in a variety of sizes and thicknesses. They were made from the soft hairs from the ears of bullocks, calves and donkeys, and the fibers and barks of certain trees. The finest brushes were made from the tail hairs of cats, muskrats, squirrels and goats. The test to determine which hairs were suitable was that the hairs should draw together when dipped in water, and should be neither too hard nor too soft.

The animal's hair was cut, then wetted and inserted through one end of a feather quill and pulled out from the other. The tips were tied to the quill and strengthened with melted shellac. Quills from the feathers of pigeons and peacocks were used depending on whether the brush required was thin or thick. For painting pearls and dots, a brush with a rounded point was used, while for tracing hair, a very fine brush, sometimes with a single hair, was used. It is interesting to note that most of these items are still manufactured and used in India in almost the same form as they were in those times.

COLOR PREPARATIONS

Pigments were obtained from minerals, and ochers and different shades were obtained from a mixture of the two. Vegetable colors included indigo, lac dye and carmine, while carbon from various sources produced black. Gold and silver powders and black and red ink were used for both writing and painting. Usually the writing was done in black and the borders in red, but certain manuscripts were written entirely in gold and silver. Reading them is a strain on the eyes, and one can only conclude that they were not meant for reading but were objects of devotion and served as a measure of the wealth of the patrons who commissioned them.

According to the *Silparatna*, a sixteenth-century Sanskrit treatise, white was obtained from burnt conch shell or white earth, while elephant apple (*Seronia elephantum*) juice and gum from the *neem* tree (*Margosa indica*) served as binding media. The same treatise gives the following recipe for obtaining black pigment. "In an earthen cup filled with oil, the wick is saturated with oil and lit. Then a globular earthen pot, with the inside besmeared with dried cow dung, is placed over the flame. The lampblack sticking to the inside of the pot should then be scraped, kneaded in an earthen pot and allowed to dry. It should be mixed with *neem* water (gum and pure water), levigated and then dried." Another recipe is to take a barley-sized grain of blue element, possibly antimony, grind it to a fine powder, mix it with *kapittha* (elephant apple) juice, and let it dry.

The various shades of red are described as soft red, medium red and deep red. These can be obtained from red lead, red ocher and shellac dye. Red ocher was extensively used in ancient paintings, and red lead was a favorite with Jain painters of western India. To get the color, white lead was roasted in an open fire until it turned a deep color. The red colored lead was then ground for half a day in water and the process repeated for twenty-four hours after five days. Gum from the *neem* tree was added to it as a binding medium.

For vermilion, crude cinnabar was thoroughly levigated in a mortar with the help of sugared water or lime juice. It was allowed to settle and the yellowish water drained off. To obtain the purest color the process was repeated fifteen times or more, after which it was again levigated with sugared water or lime juice and gum. After being thoroughly mixed, it was shaped into tablets and left to dry. To ensure that the right amount of gum had been added, the powder was examined several times during the preparation. As a test, a piece of paper was sprinkled with this cinnabar solution, folded and kept in a damp place. If the ends did not stick immediately, the preparation was right. If, after drying, the cinnabar spots on the paper flaked off when touched with the fingernails, more gum was required.

Shellac dye was used for red and was also mixed with other colors to obtain various shades. To prepare it, water was boiled while the powder of lac resin was mixed in gradually and stirred all the time to prevent the resin from solidifying. Then the temperature of the water was raised and lode and borax powders added every few minutes. Dipping a pen in the solution and drawing a few lines on paper was a simple test to see if the color was right. If the ink did not crack, the color was ready. The mixture was taken off the fire, and after the water had evaporated the residue was the color. The following proportions were used: 1/4 *seer* (1 *seer* is 2.18 lbs.) of water, 1 *tola* (80 *tolas* make a *seer*) of good dry resin of the pipal tree, known as *lakhdana*, 1/2 *tola* pathani lode and one *anna* (1/16 of a *tola*) of borax. If the shellac dye was to be used on palm leaf, then 1/4 *tola* of *madder*, a climbing plant with yellow flowers, was added to deepen the shade.

For blue, the main material used was indigo, mixed with other colors to produce various shades. Blue was also extracted from lapis-lazuli, although this was difficult since the stone contains calcite which is white and iron pyrites which has a golden sheen. Methods for extracting blue from lapis-lazuli were not known before the thirteenth century.

Orpiment was one of the minerals from which yellow was extracted. It was throughly levigated to the consistency of fine, white flour and sifted. This was again levigated with a solution of gum arabic. Another method was to boil the urine of a cow that had been fed on mango leaves for a few days. After the water had evaporated the sediment was rolled into balls which were dried first on a charcoal fire and then in the sun.

Gold, as a coloring agent, was used in India from very early times. Gold leaf was first reduced to very small pieces and then mixed with sand and water and thoroughly levigated in a smooth stone mortar. When the gold was reduced to powder, it was put in a glass cup, and the sand and dust were removed by washing. After the gold was free of impurities, it was mixed with glue and was ready for use. After the application of gold the surface of the painting was burnished with a boar's tusk to impart gloss. Another method was to first draw the design that required the application of gold, and then cut a similar design from gold leaf. This was applied to the surface and rubbed down with cotton wool.

To prepare gold and silver powders, gold or silver leaf was put in a hard stone mortar and levigated with a *dhau* (*Anogeiss latifolia*) gum solution. After the powder was ready, it was dissolved in sugared water and thoroughly stirred. When the gold powder had settled to the bottom of the solution, the water was slowly drained. This process was repeated several times until no trace of gum remained. After drying, the powder was ready for use.

For small quantities, a glass dish was smeared with *dhau* gum and the gold or silver leaf pasted on it and reduced to a powder with the fingers. It was then dissolved in sugared water and the same process repeated. The Mughal painter used honey instead of *dhau* gum. After the gold leaf was ground, water was added and the mixture strained through a finely woven cloth, being constantly stirred so that no particles settled on the strainer. The mixture was allowed to stand for fifteen hours and the water was then drained off slowly. The mouth of the basin was covered with a cloth to keep off dust particles. Size was added to this as a binding medium. The exact quantity of size required was added at one time, for if it was less, it would not stick to the painting and if it was more, it could not be burnished and the gold would lose its luster.

For making the size, the *Vishnudharmottara Purana* states: "Pieces of buffalo hide are boiled in water until they become as soft as butter. The water is then evaporated and the paste is shaped into sticks and dried in the sunshine. When required, a stick is boiled with water in a mud vessel. It fixes and tempers colors and stops them flaking." Gum from the *sindura* tree (*Carislea tomentosa*) is recommended as an astringent for the tempering of colors. In addition to the size, *neem* gum is suggested as an astringent for conch shell and oyster shell powders. In paper manuscripts, gum arabic was used for all colors, except zinc white and yellow *peori*, for which *dhau* gum served as the binding medium.

Formulae are laid down to obtain different shades by mixing colors. For example, orpiment mixed with deep brown yields the color of parrot feathers; yellow mixed with lampblack in a proportion of two to one would produce the skin color of common people; lampblack mixed with shellac dye yields deep purple; lampblack mixed with indigo yields the color of hair; red ocher mixed with conch shell lime powder yields the shade of smoke as does lampblack mixed with conch shell lime; red and yellow mixed in equal proportions yield the color of flames; zinc white and shellac dye will produce a rose color. *Jatilinga* dye, white and vermilion mixed in equal quantities yield the skin colors of members of higher castes.

As painting progressed, the old tenets were used with ever greater flexibility. In Mughal paintings the paper, after burnishing, was covered with a rough sketch made with the painted end of a charred twig of the *arhar* (*Cazanaus canzan*) plant. In the second stage the details were marked and the correct lines drawn with a mixture of lampblack and carmine, and water alone was sometimes used for the sketch. When dry it would leave a faint impression to guide the artist. Sometimes, the water was left to stand until it had completely evaporated, leaving a slight sediment which was used to tint a portrait and which contrasted well with the flesh tone of the face.

COLOR APPLICATION

After the correct outline had been drawn, the painting was covered with a thin coating of zinc that filled the pores of the paper and made it smooth and impervious to liquid colors. The final drawing was made with the aid of the outlines visible through the coating. The painting was executed with light strokes of the brush, allowing for no break or weakness in the strokes. Too firm a handling would detract from the desired quality of lightness so loved by the Mughal painter. When the picture was finished, the reverse side was then burnished. The illustrated side was placed on polished glass or a polished marble slab and burnished with an agate burnisher which imparted a mellow glow to the surface. Different color coatings were applied to the picture and after each, the burnishing process was repeated. Each color was allowed to dry completely before the next color was applied. The color coatings were always thinly applied to prevent flaking.

If, in spite of all the care taken to apply the color washes rapidly or to blend the colors together so as to avoid sharp boundaries, etc., the color distribution appeared uneven, they were removed by making a light solution of the same color and applying this to the area after first wetting it. The undesired color was removed by rubbing with a wet brush.

The order for the application of color was (1) foreground and background, (2) body colors, (3) clothes and other articles, (4) gold where required. The final outline was drawn in at the very end. The finishing touches were the painting in of pearls on ornaments and the reddening of hands, feet and lips.

To complete the picture the following steps were required: the preparation of the ground, called *zamin bandhna* by the Mughal painters; the first sketch, or *tipai*; the filling in of details, or *sachchi tipai*; light and shade modeling done with lines and dots; and the final outline and coloring.

After completion, the picture was mounted and the borders painted. These were jobs done by the *vasligar*, or mounter, and the *naqsnavis*, who painted the pattern on the borders. The calligraphy on the face or reverse of the picture was done by the *khushnavis* (calligrapher). Often the manuscript page was written first and the space for the illustration left to be painted in at a later stage. Sometimes the writing and painting stages followed each other, but quite often the written pages just lay around and were not illustrated until one hundred and fifty years or more later. This explains the discrepancies between the styles of writing and painting found in certain manuscripts.

The picture was then trimmed and mounted on stronger card. Sometimes it was placed to one side of the page and not too far from the binding. Borders were ornamented with running patterns of flowers and leaves or detached flowers repeated at intervals. Some borders were embellished with diagonal lines of writing and human and animal figures, or merely by dotting the surface with gold leaf with the bristles of a stiff brush. Elegant quotes of two or four lines of poetry, written diagonally, or a flower motif decorated the reverse. The quality of black used for painting was different from that used for writing. For the latter, the black pigment for painting was mixed with *harra* and *amla* (*Terminalia chebula* and *Phyllanthus emblica*). The black pigment was obtained by lighting a wick dipped in sesame oil and catching the soot in an earthenware receptacle. When enough had been collected, it was mixed with gum arabic to make *siyahi*, or india ink.

Even today the large number of miniatures being turned out in the country use the same techniques and roughly the same materials. The best ones, which are almost indistinguishable from the best products of earlier centuries, are also subjected to a process of ageing by exposure to the sun and smoke.

Materials and Techniques

3

The Themes

Miniature paintings in India depict a variety of themes, from the doings of gods and kings to important episodes in the lives of men. Scenes of valor and heroism, worship and devotion, lovers' trysts and partings, the holding of courts and the building of cities, all provided grist to the painter's mill. A great many of the paintings were made as book illustrations. Others served as illustrations for great works such as the *Bhagavata Purana*, compiled in south India in the tenth century in no special order and with only the most rudimentary text written at the bottom or at the top. Still others were made for keeping in folios, to be taken out and admired as and when the occasion arose, or for hanging on walls.

This body of work can be almost equally divided into religious and non-religious paintings. Even in the Jain school, where the art of painting was used for illustrating religious works, a great volume of secular painting is also included. Between the Jain and Mughal periods, that is, from the tenth to the seventeenth centuries, miniatures were also produced to illustrate cookery books and love stories, and to record the doings of kings and countries.

Perhaps the single most important branch of painting was that of portraiture. Kings and emperors used painting as the Europeans did, as a vehicle for recording the likeness of every man of note. Portraits of certain dignitaries were made at all stages of their lives, faithfully recording the transition from childhood to youth to old age. In India these miniature portraits served a very valuable purpose by leaving for posterity a visual record of most of the people instrumental in shaping its history. In order to provide future generations with a pictorial family tree, the Mughal emperor Akbar had himself painted seated in the center and surrounded by his ancestors of the Mughal dynasty. Abul Fazl, the emperor's chronicler, records that Akbar " . . . himself sat for his likeness and also ordered the portraits of all the grandees of the realm. An immense album was thus formed: those who have passed away received renewed life and those who are still alive have immortality promised them." The fashion spread to every part of the country where patronage existed for painting and innumerable portraits emerged from the painter's brush.

Similarly, all important occasions, such as the receiving of embassies, the weighing of the emperor in precious metals, the building of cities, the meeting with fakirs and ascetics, the exchanging of gifts, the listening to plaints, wars and hunts were all faithfully recorded. This, of course, was more true of the Mughal than of any other court. Jahangir had what almost amounted to a mania for having any unusual event recorded. This included the last agonies of the dying Inayat Khan, a prominent courtier, about whom Jahangir wrote that he had never seen a man look more ill and immediately sent for an artist to paint him before it was too late.

As painting moved out of the imperial ateliers to the courts of Rajasthan and the hill states, the innately hierarchical concept of Indian art asserted itself and the artist imbued each canvas he painted with a significance extending beyond the purely visual content. Love, music and religion all combined to give earthly beings a supernatural aspect and to bring the gods down to earth for the edification of mortals.

THE RAGAMALA

A whole range of paintings is found dealing with the visual depiction of musical modes and are known as the *ragamala*, "necklace of *raga*," series. (A *raga* is a selection of musical notes set in a certain progression with some more emphasized than others.) According to Indian concepts, the state of the soul is expressed by a series of sounds emanating from the throat. These, when produced by an expert, not only reflect the ultimate tensions in the singer's spirit but also evoke in the listener certain images, or rhythms, and pictorial associations with his surroundings.

Bharata Natya Shastra, the treatise on music and dance, has clearly set down the symbolism of the *ragas*, or emotions in color. The painter has taken this a step further and given visual form to the *raga* and the *ragini* (a mode of *raga* with certain omissions). All Indian music must be formulated within the limits of the *raga* and *ragini*. This is based on the belief that each *raga* or *ragani* has a sound body symbolized by a god, goddess or beautiful woman. The presiding deities of the *raga* and *ragini* are supposed to dwell in the heavenly regions, from which they can be brought to earth by the incantation of musicians.

A classification of all the *raga* and *ragini* is provided at the end of *Guru Granth Sahab*, the sacred book of the Sikhs, compiled by Guru Arjun (1581–1606). The six principal *raga* are depicted as having five wives and eight sons each, which means that the scale of twenty-two notes can be manipulated in eighty-four different ways to produce identifiably different melodies.

The six main *raga* throughout India are the same—Bhairava, Malkaus, Hindola, Deepak, Shree and Megha—but the *ragini* associated with them vary regionally. For instance, the *Granth Sahab* associates Bhairava Raga with the *ragini* Bhairavi, Bilwali, Puniyaki, Bangali and Aslekhi, while in Rajasthani music it is associated with Bhairavi, Nata Malvi, Patmanjari and Lalita. Similarly, the *Granth Sahab* associates Malkaus with Seehuti, Dhanasari, Gaundkri, Gandhari and Dev Gandhari, while the Rajputs associate it with Gauri, Khambavati, Malasari, Ramkali and Gunkali. Hindola Raga, according to the Sikhs, is associated with Telangi, Devakri, Basanti, Sandhuri and Ahiri, and according to the Rajputs, with Vilaval, Todi, Deshakhya, Dev Gandhari and Madhu Madhavi. Deepak Raga is associated with Kacheli, Patmanjari, Todi, Kamodi and Gujari among the Sikhs, and with Dhanasari, Vasant Kanahara, Varavi, and Purvi in Rajasthan; Megha is associated with Sorath, Gaurmalhari, Asa, Gunguni and Sahau in Sikh music, and Bangali, Gujri, Gaurmalhari, Kakubha and Bibhasi in Rajasthani music. Shree Raga has four wives, Bhairavi, Karnati, Gauri, and Sindhvi, according to the *Granth Sahab*, but in Rajasthan, five wives are mentioned: Pancham, Asavari, Sita Malhar, Kedar and Kumudini.

Other regions allot a different number of wives to each *raga*. Thus, in Kangra:

Bhairava has four wives: Puniyaki, Sanchi, Bilwali and Bhairavi;
Malkaus has five: Gunkali, Gandhari, Seehuti, Dev Gandhari and Dhanasari;

The Themes

35

Hindola, five   : Bhim Palasi, Ahiri, Basanti, Telangi and Sandhuri;
Deepak, five   : Gujari, Todi, Kamodi, Patmanjari and Kacheli;
Shree, four   : Vairati, Gauri, Karnati and Saveri;
Megha, five   : Sorath, Gaurmalhari, Gunguni, Suhi and Asavari.

According to the *Granth Sahab*, the sons of the *raga* are as follows:

Bhairava : Pancham, Harakh, Desakh, Bangalm, Madhu, Madhav, Lalit, Bilawal;

Malkaus : Chandhausak, Khau, Khatt, Bhaurand, Maru, Mastang, Mewar, Prabal;

Hindola : Surmanand, Bhaskar, Chandarbimb, Mangal, Sarasban, Vinod, Basant, Kamod;

Deepak : Kalanka, Kuntak, Rama, Kamalkusum, Champak, Gaura, Kannara, Kalyan;

Shree : Salu, Sarang, Sagra, Gaund, Gambhir, Gund, Kumbh, Hamir;

Megha : Vairadhar, Gajadhar, Kaidara, Jablindhar, Shankar, Shyama Nat and Jaldhara.

According to Kangra tradition, the *raga* have a different number of sons each:

Bhairava has eight : Pancham, Lalit, Bawal, Desakh, Madhava, Harakh, Bangala, and Madhu;

Malkaus, nine   : Maru, Mewar, Chammal, Dutia, Bhaurand, Shoshar, Mastang, Prabal and Kast;

Hindola, eight   : Vinod, Basant, Bhaskar, Mangal, Viveech, Surmanand, Barbal and Lahula;

Deepak, six   : Kuntak, Champak, Kalanka, Himal, Kusum and Rama;

Shree, eight   : Vardhan, Gambhir, Malava, Sarang, Behagra, Kumbh, Gaurmalhar and Achar;

Megha, seven   : Chandra, Kaidara, Shankara Bharn, Jaldhara, Kanra, Gajadhar and Nat.

Each *raga* or *ragini* is played or sung during a particular season or at a specified time of day to denote various aspects of life. The activities inspiring them probably gave them their names. Thus, the Hindola Raga must have been inspired by the swing. In the rainy season, swings are affixed to trees all over north India. Two girls stand on either side of the plank and swing, holding onto the ropes with both hands. The colorfully dressed women and girls on the plank sing songs, and the melodies match the rhythm of the swing as it soars higher and higher.

Deepak, the melody of burning light, if properly played or sung, is powerful enough to burn the body of the performer and to cause all lamps to be lit spontaneously. Tan Sen, the greatest known court singer in Indian history, was once compelled by Akbar to sing it. Knowing its power, he did this sitting in the river Jamuna. As the song reached a peak, the waters of the river began to boil. Tan Sen's body was badly burned and he became unconscious. Unable to wear any clothing, he wandered around naked until another expert musician, a young girl this time, sang the Megha Malhar, causing rain to fall in torrents and cool his body. The two *raga* are, therefore, depicted by lighted lamps and overhanging clouds.

The names of the *raga* give an idea of how they were depicted. For instance, Nat means "acrobat," and the *raga* is represented by acrobats performing feats; Hindola is denoted by the swing; Deepak by the *deepa*, or lamp; Basant by the symbols of spring; Bhairava, one of the names of the god Shiva, is shown by a symbol representing him.

Apart from the season, the *raga* are also related to different parts of the day. There is a specific *raga* and *ragini* for almost every hour of the day—Bhairava is sung before daybreak, Ramakiri at dawn, Asavari, Bhairavi and Bhilavali after sunrise, Sarang at noon, Nat and Malava in the afternoon, Kalyan in the evening and Kaidara and Chandra late at night. The full flavor of a *raga* or *ragini* is experienced only at its appointed time. To sing or play it at any other time is not only evidence of a lack of taste and knowledge, but is also considered inauspicious.

The paintings also give an idea of the time of day alloted to the *raga*. For instance, Sarang is represented in Kangra as a young girl churning curd. The burning sun and the glare give an idea of a hot noon. Chandra is represented by the moon god seated on a chariot drawn by black bucks, his body as pale as the moon; and Kaidara is shown as a young prince listening to music alone on a moonlit night.

While *raga* are depicted as male figures doing heroic feats like wrestling, drawing

The Themes

a bow or galloping on horseback, *ragini* are female figures expressing sentiments of love, whether in fulfillment or in separation.

As the *ragini* associated with the *raga* differ from place to place, their depiction is also different. In Rajasthan, Asavari Ragini is visualized as a young woman playing the snake-charmer's flute to bring down the snakes from the sandalwood tree; in Kangra it is depicted as a young woman seated on a low stool, smelling a flower, while an old woman stands beside her holding jasmine flowers. In Rajasthan, Dhanasari Ragini is represented as a young woman crying as she paints the portrait of her absent husband for whom she is pining; in Kangra she sits on a carpet fondling a pair of rabbits while her husband is shown in the background riding home.

The Krishna cult also had an influence on *ragamala* paintings and often the male figure in the *raga* is Krishna himself. He dances alone or with women, as in Basant Raga, and is the lover who comes back in the early hours of the morning in Lalita Ragini.

Some of the *raga* and *ragini* are associated with religion and represent worship. The Bhairava Raga, Shankara Bharn Raga and Bhim Palasi Ragini represent the worship of Shiva the Destroyer, the third figure in the Hindu trinity. The Ragini is represented as a young, bare-bosomed woman worshiping the *lingam*, symbol of Shiva.

The earliest *ragamala* painting is met with in Jain manuscripts, although its real growth dates from the sixteenth century at the courts of Baz Bahadur of Mandu and Ibrahim Adil Shah of Bijapur, both great lovers of music and painting.

The Rajput and Pahari painters also produced large quantities of work on this theme. Rajasthani *ragamala* paintings are imbued with passion, to which the strongly vibrant colors are a contributing feature, expressing both joy and sorrow. Those produced in the Pahari schools are much more sober and restrained, and have a dreamlike quality which is very soothing to the eye but does not strike any strong chord in the viewer.

Animals and birds are used to highlight the symbolism of the paintings and help to establish the sober, joyous, playful or lovelorn moods. Peacocks, pigeons, deer, rabbits, donkeys, love birds, hawks, gazelles, snakes, bulls, *saras* cranes and, of course, horses are all seen in *ragamala* paintings. Monkeys are a favorite in Rajasthan, but are completely absent in paintings from the hill states in the north.

NAYIK NAYIKA

The *nayika*, or heroines of the ancient Indian writers, were young women preoccupied with love in its different forms. They were divided into eight different categories.

Svadhinapatika: or "she who dominates her beloved." In the miniatures the woman is depicted with the *nayik*, "hero," massaging or washing her feet or putting the vermilion mark on her forehead.

Utkanthita: the heroine is alone and yearns for her lover, who has been inadvertently delayed from keeping the tryst. She is depicted sitting on a bed of leaves at the edge of a forest pool while wild deer roam nearby.

Basakasayya: she awaits her lover by her bed, and is depicted either welcoming him or waiting for him at the door while her maids prepare the bed.

Abhisandhita: she is separated from her lover owing to her own ill temper or lack of consideration. The hero is usually shown walking away from her in a dejected mood.

Khandita: she is offended and is usually seen reproaching her lover for his lack of faithfulness.

Prositapatika: she sits and mourns the departure of her lover surrounded by her maids, and refuses to be consoled.

Vipralabdha: she is shown throwing away her jewels because her lover has failed to keep the tryst.

Abhisarika: she braves the storm and lightning, snakes and other dangers of the forest to meet her lover. She is usually shown at the door of her house or on the way to the tryst. Trying to blend in with her surroundings, she wears white garments on moonlit nights and dark ones when the night is stormy.

The *nayik*, or hero, can also be categorized into the following types.

Pati	:	the husband.
Upapati	:	the paramour as Krishna is with Radha.
Vaisika	:	the ladies' man well acquainted with the ways of women.
Satha	:	the false and heartless lover.
Manisatha	:	the false lover enraged at the rejection of his false protestations.

The Themes

Dharista : the hero who has neither shame nor pity.

Often the *nayik* is depicted as Krishna himself and the *nayika* as Radha.

The go-betweens are as important as the heroes and heroines. Women go-betweens are classified as *dutika*, or "messenger," and *sakhi*. The former is a friend or handmaiden of the heroine and the latter is a constant companion and friend. The hero has to enlist their aid to get the ear of his beloved.

The *ragamala* theme became intertwined with the *nayik-nayika* theme and this resulted in paintings that could be depictions of either. The *basakasayya nayika*, for instance, who prepares the bed for her lover, is hardly distinguishable from the Kakubha Ragini, who holds two garlands for her returning lover. Similarly, the Bangala Ragini goes to the forest to do penance for the return of her lover as does the *prositapatika nayika*. Like the *svadhinapatika nayika*, the Vairadi Ragini dominates her lover by her charms. The maiden depicted as Desa Varati Ragini is really a heroine pining for her lover.

THE SEASONS

Indians live very close to nature and the change of seasons never fails to fascinate them. Poets and writers have described this phenomenon with an ecstasy bordering on the mystic. The *Baramasa*, the twelve months of the year, has been depicted in prose, verse and painting in loving detail and never fails to delight readers and viewers.

The *Baramasa* of the sixteenth-century poet, Kesava Das, has enriched Hindi literature with its delightful account of the life of the people and the rituals and ceremonies of the various seasons. The seventh-century Sanskrit poet and playwright, Kalidasa, in his *Ritusamhara* and *Meghdoot* has given descriptions of the seasons that are seldom surpassed anywhere in the world. The *Baramasa* has been given visual life especially by the Rajput and Pahari painters.

During springtime, the land is covered with the gold of the mustard flowers. The scarlet and orange flowers of the flame of the forest (*dhak*) and *asoka* (*Saraca indica*) trees give vivid life to the landscape, with the mauve blossoms of the *kachnar*, or bauhinia, and the pale yellow flowers of the mango providing counterpoint, which helps to keep the exuberance in check. The great festival of Holi,

1. *Pala.* Late 11th century. Death of Buddha—detail from a palm leaf manuscript. The drawing is extremely fine and, in spite of the small space available, detailed. There is a sense of peaceful serenity that is entirely missing from Jain miniatures.

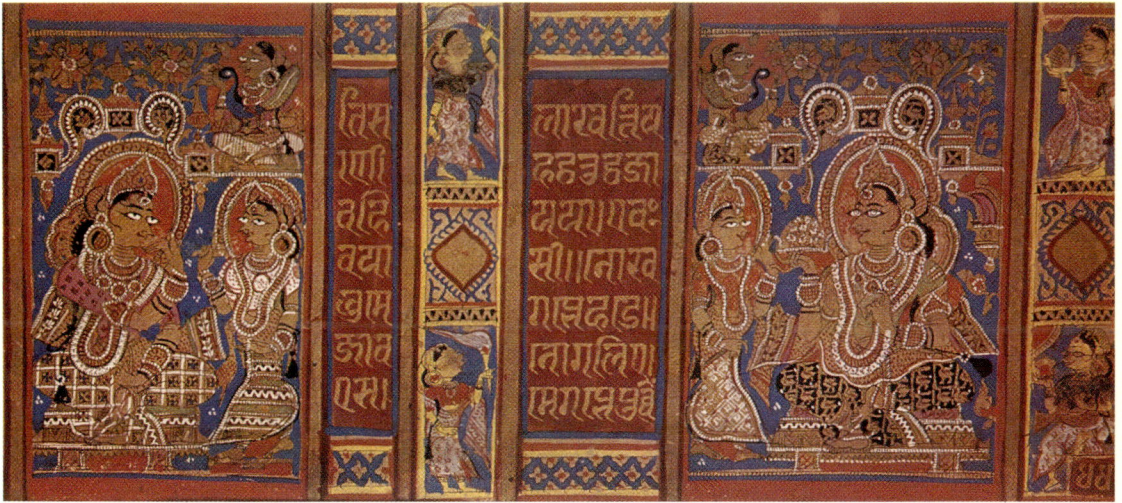

2. *Jain.* Late 15th century. Mothers of the Tirthankaras. The typical Jain colors of ultramarine and Indian red give a most decorative appeal to the picture. Note the rounded chests and the halos. The drawing is much bolder than that of plate 41, and the protruding eye, sharp nose and double chin are prominent.

3. *Rajasthan*. Late 15th century. Economy of line is used here to produce maximum effect. The eye is large but no longer protrudes. Colors are subdued but used well, and the composition is marked with a strong folk flavor.

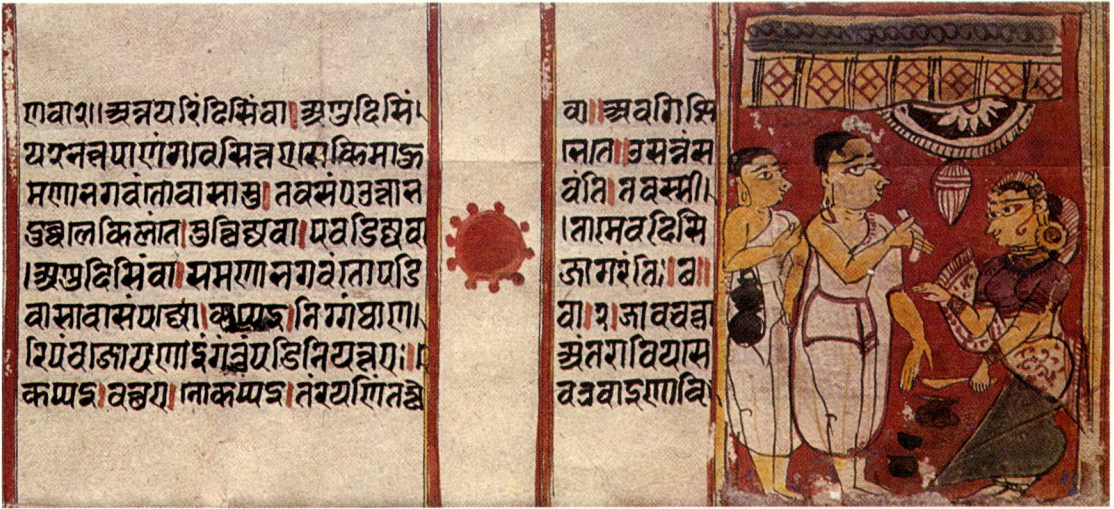

4. *Jain.* 17th century. All the early Jain characteristics are there—the protruding eye, sharp nose and double chin—but the lines are much bolder and there is no use of gold in the elementary colors. The figures are not drawn proportionately: the left arm of the central figure is distorted and the female figure is disproportionate.

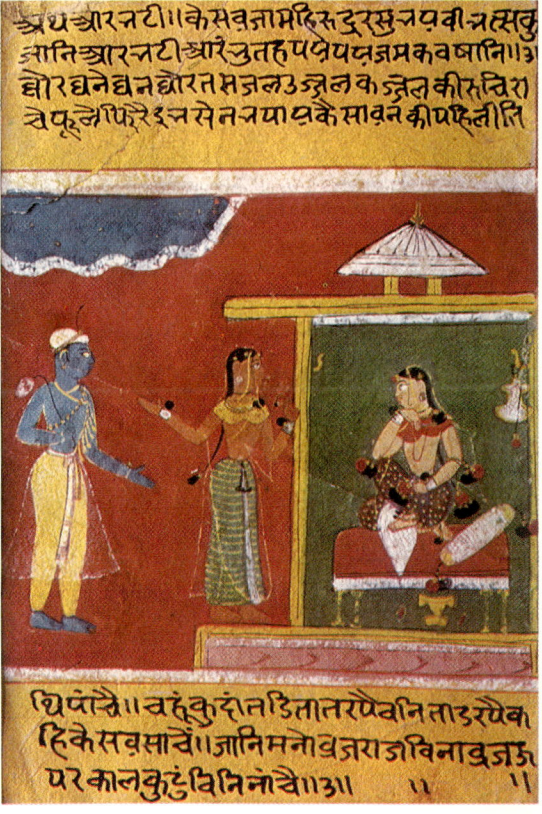

5. *Malwa.* Middle 17th century. The eye has now shrunk to normal proportions, but it is still the most prominent feature of the face, the whites being greatly emphasized. Gauzy draperies are mostly indicated by the line drawn around the body, but sometimes, as in the case of the figure on the left, a touch of white is also used. Economy of line and a judicious use of color strengthen the composition.

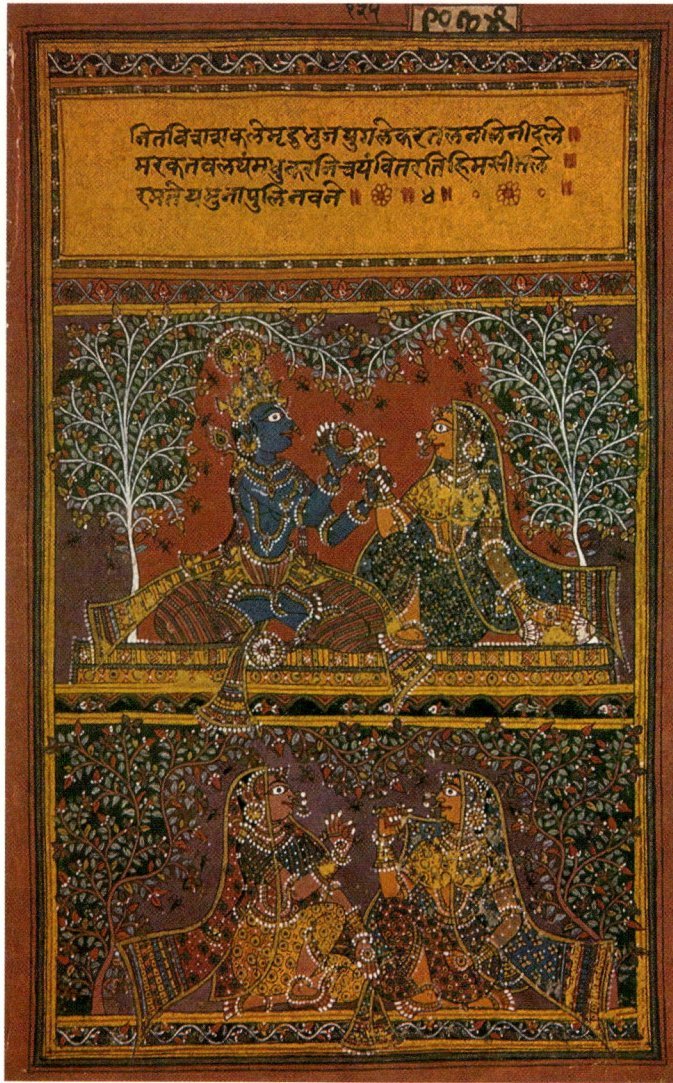

नितविवादक ...
मरकतवलयम् ...
रसले ... नवने

6. *Orissa.* Late 18th or early 19th century. This is a meeting ground of many influences: the stiff stance, the protruding eye and the projecting ornaments are obviously Malwa, but the colors used are from Rajasthan. The swirling draperies and profusion of flowering trees and vines give an air of fantasy to the composition.

7. *Mughal.* Late 16th century. A page from the *Babarnamah.*
The entire area teams with rearing horses and fighting men.
The gold and colors so beloved by the Persians are present,
along with the caparisoned horses which resemble those of
medieval Europe. However, the Middle Eastern warriors are
battling in an undoubtedly Indian landscape.

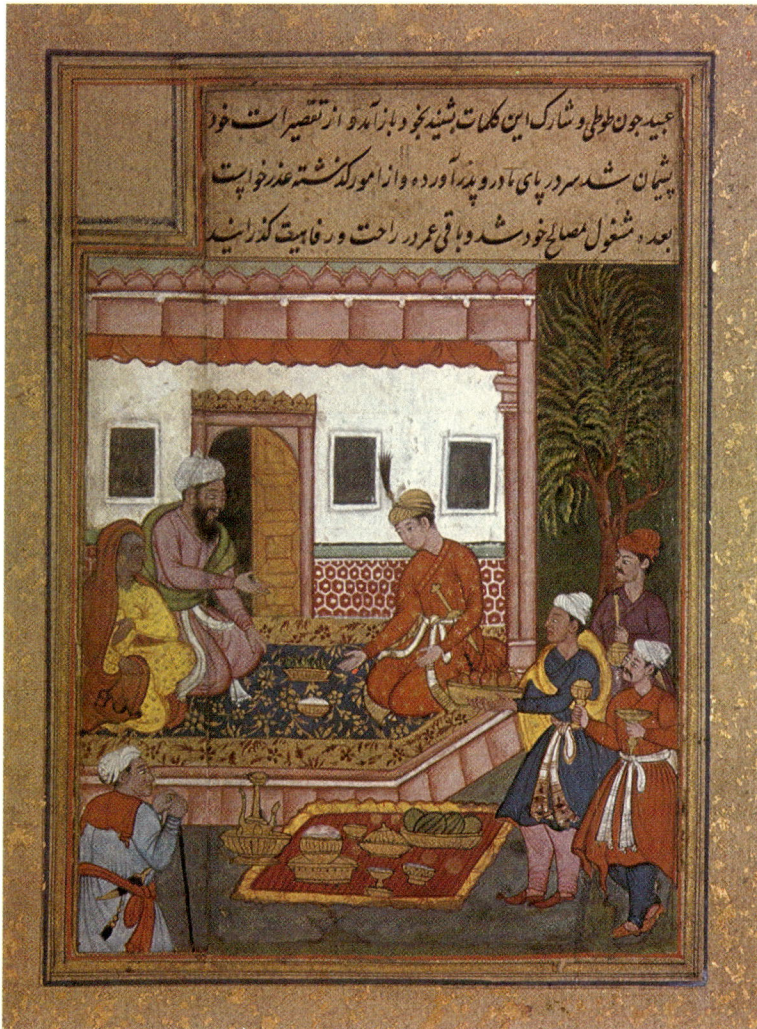

8. *Mughal.* Late 16th or early 17th century. The drawing is extremely
fine, the colors deep, though subdued, and there is a restrained use of
gold. The faces of the two main figures as well as the figures on the right
are Mongol, while the female figure is totally Indian. One man wears a
four-pointed *jama,* and the rest wear circular skirts. The gold stippling
around the picture is meant to highlight the colors in the painting.

9. *Provincial Mughal.* Late 16th century. This *Ramayana* episode depicts the battle between the monkey and demon armies outside the gates of Lanka. The figures are not as finely drawn as in the 17th century. The Persian influence is mostly discernible in the architecture, but both the subject and its treatment are entirely Indian. The picture was probably painted at one of the Rajput courts that were greatly influenced by the Mughals.

10. *Mughal.* Early 17th century. Emperor Jahangir at the hunt. A lion that has been killed is being put on the back of an elephant. Note the fine brushstrokes, the deep perspective, the sense of movement and the natural atmosphere. The pastel shades with touches of dark color impart an aristocratic elegance to the picture.

11. *Mughal.* Early 17th century. A Jesuit priest. Note that the European clothes and features are handled in a typically Indian way by the Mughal painter. The landscape in the background adds depth to the picture.

12. *Mughal.* Middle 17th century. This is one of the finest examples of portraiture. The transparent fabric revealing the flesh tones of the subject, the finely molded face and the the expressive hands are all typical of this period.

13. *Mughal.* Late 18th century. Prince enjoys himself at the festival of Holi in the harem. The decorated clothes, the pavilion and poppy beds are in the usual court style, but the stripes of color in the foreground impart a folk look to the picture.

14. *Mughal.* Early 18th century. *Rakshasa* (evil spirit) riding an elephant
made up of numerous animals including a man. The whole is very
cleverly worked so that the components become integral parts of the
elephant. The snake forms the trunk and top of the head, and the
leopard part of the back and tail. Such composite animals (some were
made up entirely of women) were painted in many places.

15. *Ahmadnagar.* Middle 16th century. Patahansika Ragini. The stiffly swirling draperies are typical of this school and bear a strong resemblance to the sarees worn in the area today. The coloring and the decoration are Persian, but the rest is undoubtedly Indian.

16. *Deccan*. Early 17th century. Krishna with *gopis*. The female figures are typically Deccan although they are also featured in Mughal painting, depicted usually as serving women. The Chinese cloud formation is a frequent feature of Deccan paintings, but the architecture and the main figure are Rajasthani. The picture was probably painted in one of the Hindu courts of the Deccan.

17. *Deccan*. Late 17th century. Portrait of a nobleman. The picture lacks the character insight that Mughal paintings depicted so well and is a straightforward likeness of the subject. The ornamental shrubs in the foreground, the wispy clouds and the sash are typically Deccan.

18. *Bijapur.* Middle 17th century. The Mughal influence has become stronger, with underarm shading exaggerated to the point where it covers both shoulders. The picture has been damaged, but traces of the typical Deccan ornamented foreground and curly clouds are still visible.

19. *Deccan*. Late 18th century. Lady at her toilette. This is an interesting picture for the variety of faces shown. The face of the figure on the left bears a strong resemblance to faces found in Kishangarh, while the others are Mughal and Rajput. The porcelain quality of the skin of the main figure was given to portraits of the late Mughal period. Such scenes of pleasure are common during the later period of all schools.

20. *Deccan*. Late 18th century. Girl smoking a hookah. The foreground decorated with sprigs of flowers and the profusely ornamented borders are offset by the plain background and the comparative simplicity of the figure.

21. *Deccan*. Early 19th century. Emperor Shah Jahan on an elephant. The rider's stance, the modeling of the elephant, the elementary background and the halo are all evidence of the late date of the picture. The design of the covering on the elephant's back is well worked, but it does not hang naturally.

22. *Mewar*. Late 17th century. King hunting with a falcon. The simplicity of early Mewar painting is considerably toned down here.
The ornamental foreground, the subdued colors and decorated
clothes all show strong Mughal influence.

23. *Mewar*. Dated 1750, drawn by Nuruddin. Maharana Jagat Singh hunting bison. This is one of the few pictures with the date and artist's name inscribed. The old individuality of the Mewar school is gone and the picture is indistinguishable from any other product of a Rajasthani school.

24. *Rajasthan.* Middle 18th century. Painting on cloth. The picture is much bigger and bolder than it would have been had it been done on paper. The fine modeling, the depiction of individual characteristics, the apparent tension between the king and the lady on the left, and the deft handling of color all point to execution at a period when the art was at its peak.

25. *Bikaner*. Middle 18th century. A king hawking. This picture has the turbulent activity often found in early Mughal miniatures, but the variety of birds covering the sky in a haphazard manner is unique. In spite of the hectic activity there is a delicate quality to the picture partly due to the color of the middle background. The stolid soldiers in the right-hand corner balance the frenetic activity in the upper left.

26. *Bundi.*, Middle 18th century. Prince and princess hunting. Although there is a lot of movement and a sense of urgency as the princess tries to retrieve her bow from around the neck of the deer, the whole effect is marred by the filled-in surfaces. The tears falling from the eyes of the deer, white ovals, and the posture of the dead deer are both unnatural. The flaming sky with curling clouds and the lush green of the picture give it an ornamental effect.

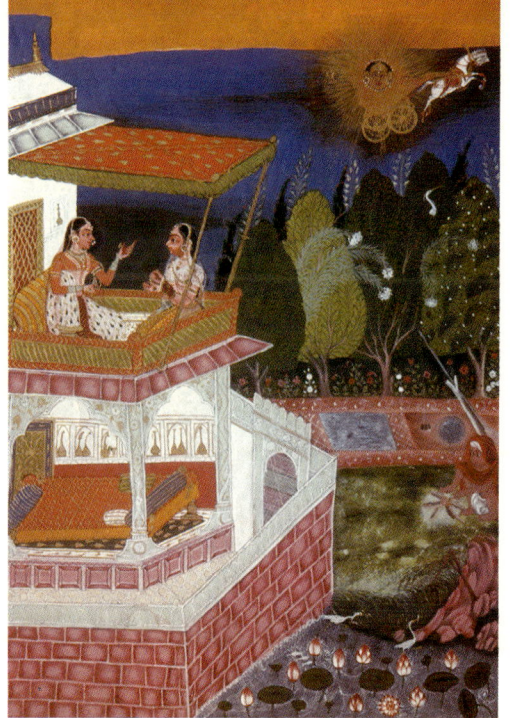

27. *Bundi.* Late 18th century. Present here are all the late Bundi characteristics: ruddy faces, a pond full of flowering lotuses, exuberant colors, lush foliage and an over-decorated look.

28. *Bundi*. Second quarter of 19th century. Apart from the action in the center of the picture, the entire border is filled with scenes of hunting, wrestling, etc. This was a favorite device used by later painters for embellishing pictures.

29. *Basohli*. Late 17th century. The proud stance of
the figures, the high foreheads, the prominent eyes
and flower-shaped trees are all Basohli characteristics. The bright color of the man's clothes makes him
prominent.

30. *Basohli school, from Nurpur.* Early 18th century. The style, with vibrant colors, large eyes and sloping foreheads, is based on early Basohli, but the extreme angularity and elongation of the figures has been replaced by rounded faces and natural proportions.

31. *Pahari, Mandi.* Raja Shamsher Sen (1727–81). The color of the raja's clothes is typical of Mandi art. The primitive quality of the drawing is obvious both in the unnatural flattening of the women's heads and the fore-shortening of the main figure.

32. *Pahari, Guler.* Middle 18th century. The maiden wails as her lover is taken away. The two parts of the picture are connected by the sorrowing girl. The sense of abandonment is heightened by the fleeing camel and the two guards striding purposefully alongside. The bright colors in the foreground focus attention on the area of action.

33. *Kangra school*. Late 18th century. Radha and Krishna in an amorous pose. The picture is undoubtedly Pahari, but there is no clear indication of provenance. The amorous mood is heightened by the excessive use of gold and the lushness of the flora and fauna although, as is usual in such scenes, the main characters seem totally detached from their actions.

34. *Kangra*. Late 18th century. Khandita Nayika—the heroine who up-
braids her errant lover. Even in anger the lady's face is a study in dulcet
charm. Like all Kangra women she is incapable of being anything but
sweetly feminine no matter how provoked.

35. *Kangra school, from Garhwal.* Late 18th century. Radha and Krishna looking into a mirror. The open look on the faces of the women, their thick tress-
es, the pond full of lotuses, the flowering shrubs, the stark trees in the background all indicate that this painting comes from Garhwal.

36. *Kangra school, from Bilaspur.* Late 18th century.
Krishna eating with the cowherds. The huge, gnarled
tree, the cattle, the sidelocks of the men are all typical
of Bilaspur painting, although here the men wear
loincloths instead of the shorts usually depicted in
miniatures of this area.

37. *Kishangarh*. Late 18th century. Krishna drawing Radha to bed. The picture is unmistakeably from Kishangarh judging from the facial features of the figures, the flora and fauna, and the colors.

38. *Pahari school, from Kulu*. Late 18th century. The trees, figures and animals arranged in vertical lines produce a very strong effect, while the subtle greens in the foliage highlight the vivid colors of the clothes.

39. *Kangra.* Late 18th century. An episode from the *Mahabharata.* In the rocky citadel of Shiva and his family, Ganesh stands at the edge of the cliff poised to kill the many-headed demon moving up toward the top. The rolling clouds and the flutter of Ganesh's *dhoti* give movement to the picture. Also the vibrant colors, the faces and the general composition make this one of the finest examples of this school.

40. *Sikh idiom of the Kangra school.* The sensuous atmosphere is heightened by the elaborate surroundings and the efforts of the attendants to add to the pleasure of the occupants on the bed. The style is Kangra, but the deportment of the women makes it obvious that it does not belong to the main school. The male figure is undoubtedly Sikh.

in which men and women sing songs of spring, throw colored water at one another and smear each other's faces with *gulal*, a red vegetable dye mixed with mica, signals the end of spring and the advent of summer.

During summer the heat beats down on the plains, and the trees sprout new leaves to provide shade from the scorching sun. The hot winds bring sand and dust, and even wild animals hide in caves while elephants trumpet and seek refuge in water. The scarlet and orange flowers of the *gulmohar* (*Delonix regia*) and the golden yellow of the laburnum, or *amaltas*, trees help to heighten the blazing quality of the landscape.

After summer come the monsoons. The heavens open and water pours down in torrents on the parched earth, covering it with a carpet of green grass. This, with the patter of falling rain, provides the ideal background for lovers' trysts, for the rainy season in India is imbued with eroticism. Poets write about the wife lamenting her husband's absence and cringing at the sight of the empty bed on which she must sleep alone. It is such a wife's lament that forms the subject matter of Kalidasa's *Meghdoot*. Seeing a cloud in the sky, the wife asks it to go and find her husband and tell him of her loneliness. The poet recounts the cloud's odyssey, thus displaying an amazing knowledge of the country and the people inhabiting it. This is also the month when swings are hung under trees and women clad in brilliant red and green clothes fill their leisure hours with swinging and singing.

The end of the rains and the beginning of winter is heralded by the festivals of Dussehra and Deepavali. Dussehra is celebrated for different reasons in different parts of the country, but in the north of India it is celebrated as the day on which Rama returned to Ayodhya after fourteen years in exile. The occasion is marked by fireworks and general festivity. Twenty days after Dussehra comes Deepavali, the festival of lights, when lamps glitter all over the country. Even the poorest house has a small lamp burning in front of it to show Lakshmi, goddess of wealth, the way, so that the inhabitants of the house can benefit from her munificence throughout the year. According to the Hindu calendar, Deepavali is the darkest night of the year. Winter comes into the plains bringing a blaze of flowers of various kinds and a thinning of the leaves on trees to let the pale sunshine touch the earth. Fires are lit in the open, and around them men and women sit, exchanging gossip or recounting tales. The hills are covered with snow and life moves indoors.

The Themes

LOVE STORIES

Certain love stories caught the imagination of the artists and appear in miniature paintings of different schools.

LAILA AND MAJNU

This Persian love story is in the style of Romeo and Juliet. Majnu, the son of a chieftain, is in love with Laila, the daughter of the chief of a rival clan. His craving for her leads him to madness, and eventually, when Laila comes to him, he flees from her and she dies of grief. During his search for Laila, he roams the desert and wild animals gather around him. In the city he is derided and children throw stones at him. He is usually depicted as an emaciated young man, scantily clad and with disheveled hair.

NALA AND DAMAYANTI

This tale is part of the *Mahabharata*. Damayanti, the beautiful daughter of the king of Vidarbha falls in love with King Nala. On the day of her *svayamvara*, when she is to choose a husband, the gods Indra, Agni, Varuna and Yama decide to play a trick on her by appearing as Nala. She sees five Nalas seated side by side. In despair she prays to the gods, who assume their original shapes, allowing Damayanti to place a garland around the neck of the real Nala, signifying her choice of him for a husband. Later Nala gambles away his kingdom and has to go into exile as a beggar. Damayanti follows him, but he deserts her. Finally, after many trials the lovers are united and the kingdom regained.

This story is a favorite especially of the Pahari school. Pictures dealing with the honeymoon period are frankly, though tenderly, erotic.

DHOLA AND MARU

There was a famine in Poongal around the tenth century A.D. Raja Pingal goes with his family to Narwan, where Raja Nala welcomes him heartily. Nala's son, Dhola, is liked by Pingal's *rani*, who marries him to her young daughter, Marwan, affectionately called Maru. When Dhola is older he is married to Malwan, a princess of Malwa, who does not know of his earlier marriage. Maru sees him in a dream and becomes obsessed with a desire to meet him. After many difficulties she finds him, despite Malwan putting many obstacles in her way. Finally, the two wives start living together amicably. It is a universally known epic in Rajasthan, where it is regarded as the ideal husband-wife relationship. It is sung and recited all over the area, and consists of thousands of couplets.

Since the area in which this episode takes place is mostly desert, the lovers together, or Dhola alone, are either depicted on camelback or dismounting from a camel, or with the camel waiting for them outdoors.

SONI AND MAHIVAL

This is a tale of a Punjabi girl, Soni, who loved a buffalo herder, Mahival. Every night Soni crossed the river to meet her lover, using an inverted earthenware pot as a float. One night her brothers, infuriated by her dalliance, substituted a pot of unbaked clay for the one she always used. The pot disintegrated in midstream, and Soni, who could not swim, drowned. This story was popular with Pahari painters and was even painted by Mughal artists.

Stories of chivalry and the courage of Rajput princes also form the subject matter of a large number of Rajput and certain Pahari miniatures. How little the Rajputs valued life for its own sake and how dear courage and gallantry were to their hearts is illustrated by what Prithvi Raj Chauhan's wife said to him on the eve of battle. "Oh, sun of the Chauhans, none has drunk so deeply both of glory and pleasure as thou. Life is like an old garment. What matter if we throw it off? To die well is life immortal."

THE MAHABHARATA

The *Mahabharata* and the *Ramayana* (see p. 83) are the two great epics of India. The central theme of the *Mahabharata* is the great battle fought on the field of Kurukshetra between two sets of cousins—the one hundred Kauravas and the five Pandavas, symbolizing evil against good. It has always fired the imagination of poets and painters and its many incidents have been reproduced in a myriad ways.

Kunti, the mother of the Pandavas, was the daughter of a nymph and the sister of Vasudeva, the father of Krishna. By virtue of a boon she received from a sage, she could have five children by any god she chose. She already had one son by the worship of Surya, the sun god. This was Karna, whose birth she concealed,

The Themes

and who was brought up elsewhere. Her husband, Pandu, due to a curse, was unable to consort with his wives, and so by worshiping Dharma (Righteousness) she had Yudhisthira, by Vayu (Wind), she had Bhima, and by Indra (the king of the Heavens), she had Arjuna. The fifth boon she shared with a co-wife, who bore twin sons, Nakul and Sahadeva.

On Pandu's death, his brother Dhritarashtra took charge of the boys and brought them up with his own one hundred sons, who were known as Kauravas, from Kuru, their ancestor. The Kauravas, especially Duryodhana, became jealous of their cousins, and the rivalry became more pronounced after Dhritarashtra formally nominated Yudhisthira as his heir.

To mark the end of the boys' education, a tournament was held, and the Pandavas, especially Arjuna, displayed superior skill in the use of arms. Single combat with clubs, too, between Bhima and Duryodhana took a serious turn and the cousins had to be separated by Drona, their instructor. Karna, disguised as a Brahmin, challenged Arjuna to single combat. He had learnt the military arts from Parasurama, the avatar of Vishnu, whose purpose was to humble the Kshatriyas. On learning of the deception, Parasurama cursed Karna to ultimate defeat and death through the wrong use of a weapon. Kunti recognized her son, but to all others he was merely the son of Adhiratha, Dhritarashtra's charioteer, and could not fight a prince. But Duryodhana, enraged at Arjuna's public success, persuaded the king to confer the kingdom of Anga on Karna so that the two could fight as equals. Bhima insulted Karna while Duryodhana defended him, and the contest broke up in disorder.

As a fee for educating the boys, Drona asked his pupils to bring forth Drupada, the king of Panchalas with whom he had an old dispute, in chains. The Kauravas failed to do this, but Arjuna, with the help of his brothers, captured Drupada. Drona demanded half his kingdom from the captive king. Drupada was forced to agree, but he begged for Brahma's help and was granted the boon of a son, who would kill Drona, and a daughter, who would marry Arjuna. These were Dhrishtadyumna and Draupadi.

In the meanwhile Duryodhana prevailed upon his father to let him ascend the throne in place of Yudhisthira and to kill the Pandavas by setting their house on fire. Forewarned, the brothers escaped and went with their mother to live in the forest disguised as Brahmins. Hearing of an archery contest that was to be held for the hand of Draupadi, the Pandavas decided to attend the display. They watched as hundreds of princes failed to shoot the allotted five arrows through a ring. Karna seemed on the point of winning, when Draupadi announced she would not marry the son of a charioteer. Karna, now sure of his paternity, could not prove it and had to retire. Arjuna, looking like an unkempt Brahmin, shot the five arrows in quick succession through the ring. The humiliated princes rebelled but the Pandava brothers threw off their disguise and put them to flight.

Arjuna went to his mother and told her that he had won a great prize. Without hearing what it was, Kunti said he must share it with his brothers and so Draupadi became the wife of all five brothers, spending two days with each in turn.

Duryodhana and Karna now thought of ways of getting rid of the Pandavas. Karna was for open warfare but Duryodhana favored a plot. Drona, however, offered a compromise—that the kingdom be divided in two. This was agreed to and the Pandavas returned home. They made their capital city, Indraprastha (now Delhi), into a marvelous place with a magnificent palace and invited the Kauravas to see it. This only fanned the flames of jealousy and Duryodhana challenged Yudhisthira to a game of dice. Thanks to the skill of Sakuni, an uncle of Duryodhana and a great cheater, Yudhisthira began to lose steadily. He lost his kingdom, his brothers and his wife Draupadi. Duryodhana now called upon his brother Dussasana to humiliate Draupadi by publicly disrobing her, but she prayed to the gods and the folds of her saree became infinite, so that no matter how much they pulled, her body remained covered.

Again dice were thrown. The loser was to retire with his people for twelve years into the forest and live unrecognized in the city during the thirteenth year. Yudhisthira lost again and went into exile. The Pandavas met with many adventures during their thirteen years of exile. They formed alliances and Arjuna married Krishna's sister. In the meanwhile, the Kauravas had also found allies, and when Krishna went to them asking for the restoration of his brother-in-law's kingdom, he was attacked.

War was declared. Krishna was claimed by both sides. He offered the choice of himself unarmed or an army. The Kauravas chose the latter and Krishna became Arjuna's charioteer. Kunti tried to stop Karna from fighting against his brothers, but his debt of gratitude to Duryodhana was too great and he aligned himself with the Kauravas.

The Themes

Doubts about the war existed on both sides, but Drona and Karna repaid their debt to the Kauravas by fighting for them even though they recognized their cause as unjust. Arjuna also did not relish fighting his cousins and shedding the blood of thousands, but Krishna, revealing his identity as an incarnation of Vishnu, explained to him the necessity to fulfill one's *dharma*, or "duty." There comes a time to fight and kill, and at such a time one must not allow qualms of conscience to stand in the way of duty.

The battle was fought with courage and some trickery. For instance, the Pandavas, after fighting Drona for five days, spread the rumor that his son was dead. Since it had been prophesied that no harm would come to Aswathaman, the son, so long as his father lived, Drona did not believe the rumor until he heard it confirmed by Yudhisthira who never told a lie. Bhima had killed an elephant named Aswathaman so Yudhisthira could reply in the affirmative. Drona retired from the struggle and was killed by Draupadi's brother, Dhrishtadyumna.

Gradually all the generals and troops were killed, leaving only Duryodhana, Aswathaman and two others. Duryodhana was hurt but not killed, and planned further trickery, giving permission to Aswathaman, Drona's son, to avenge his father's death. Aswathaman propitiated Shiva, who entered his body and killed all the men in the Pandava camp, including Draupadi's five sons. He brought their heads to Duryodhana, who died at the sight.

The Pandavas themselves escaped and returned to Hastinapur, the capital, and were reconciled with their uncle, Dhritarashtra, who later retired to the forest and died in a fire.

The epic ends with all those who had upheld their *dharma* being united in heaven irrespective of which side they had fought for.

The Gods of Mythology

Without some knowledge of the concepts of Hinduism and Hindu mythology, it is not really possible to understand a great deal of painting, especially of the Pahari and Rajput schools. Even in the Mughal school such knowledge comes in handy for understanding, for example, the paintings of the *Razmnamah*, the Persian translation of the *Mahabharata*.

Hindu mythology is extremely rich and ancient, with therefore many versions of each tale and incident. For instance, how the elephant-headed god, Ganesh, came to be the way he is is explained in a variety of ways. The epics are full of episodes fraught with tenderness, romance, cunning, valor and melodrama of a high order. They have been recited and sung, with local variations, all over the country for centuries.

To the Indian artist, the stories are not impersonal events that may or may not have taken place. On the contrary, they form the essence of his very life and thought, and thus he brings all the cunning of his craft to impart to them a feeling of life and urgency.

The intimate association between the Indian and his gods has brought the great forces of life and nature within the scope of comprehension. The gods are not above men, incomprehensible and unapproachable, but share the weaknesses and foibles of mortals, becoming one with them. Even the terrible Shiva, whose dancing feet and sounding drum are the signal for the Apocalypse, is not immune to the temptations of beautiful women. He may resent his weakness and vent his anger by destroying those near him, but the weakness exists and, to that extent, he is not totally invincible. Gods can also be ousted from their abode by men who have practiced great austerities and who share their godliness. Gods, thus, face the same uncertainties—not to the same extent, of course—as men and have to stoop to connivance and trickery to maintain their power and prestige.

With all this wealth of stories, anecdotes, incidents and doings of gods, men and animals at his command, it is no wonder that the Indian painter could not find adequate satisfaction in what he saw in the world around him. No matter how rich his surroundings, the world of the supernatural, with its legend and mythology, with its inhabitants engaged in superheroic feats of love or war, could not be approximated.

Indian miniature painting, from its inception to the present time, abounds in the stories of these happenings, which tested men and gods to the limits of their endurance and laid down behavior patterns that have made Indian society what it is today.

An outline of the main gods, goddesses and legends is given briefly below. The regional variations of these legends are not included, but it is hoped that even a broad outline of them will enable the reader to identify more accurately and appreciate more fully the miniature paintings of India.

The Themes

79

SHIVA

The supreme deity manifests itself in three aspects—as the Creator, Preserver and Destroyer. These are embodied in Hindu mythology in the form of Brahma the Creator, Vishnu the Preserver and Shiva the Destroyer. The most powerful of these is Shiva, who is said to have derived his powers from the practice of austerities. He is often depicted as a *yogi* with a white face and matted hair, and dressed in a tiger skin. As the demon slayer, he is depicted in the famous *nataraja* dance pose, where he is about to kill an *asura*, or demon. He broke the force of the fall of the river Ganges as it descended the mountains in great torrents by standing beneath the waters, which wound their way through his matted locks and divided into the seven holy rivers of India. He is sometimes depicted with a blue throat, acquired as a result of churning the ocean of milk to produce *amrit*, or ambrosia, to help the gods in their struggle against demons. The serpent Vasuki, who was being used by the gods as a churning rope, spat out poison which would have contaminated the ambrosia had not Shiva caught it in his mouth. He was prevented from swallowing it by his wife Parvati, who pressed hard on his throat to hold the poison there, causing his throat to turn blue. He is often represented with five faces, three eyes and four arms. The third eye is closed because of its power to destroy— whoever it gazes upon is burnt to death. His other weapons of destruction are a trident, symbol of lightning, a sword, a bow and a club with a skull at the end, three serpents, one coiled in his piled-up hair with its hood raised above his head, one on his shoulder about his neck and one, which is his sacred thread, that goes over his right shoulder and under his left arm. In his most fearsome aspect as a destroyer for the sake of destruction, Shiva wears a garland of skulls, while as an upholder of justice, he carries a drum and a rope with which to bind sinners. The *lingam*, symbol of male energy, is often the only representation of the god, and the bull Nandi, a universal symbol of fertility, his vehicle.

Shiva likes to dance in joy, anger and sorrow, and his dancing symbolizes the movement of the universe. By dancing he destroys in order to create anew. It is the state of the cosmic truth that matter must change form from time to time to keep the universe fresh and alive.

BRAHMA

Brahma is considered to have been self-created, but with creation his main role is over, and he lacks the fiery quality of Shiva or the gentle benevolence of Vishnu. He is considered the god of wisdom, and the four *vedas*, or scriptures, are supposed to have sprung from his four heads. He has four arms and carries the *vedas* and his scepter, or a spoon and a string of beads or a bow and a water jug. His wife, Saraswati, is the goddess of music and learning; and his vehicle is a swan or a goose.

VISHNU

Vishnu, as the Preserver, is the embodiment of mercy and goodness, the all-pervading power which preserves and maintains the rhythm of the universe and the cosmic order. He is an object of devotion rather than of fear. His wife, Lakshmi, is the goddess of good fortune. He has four arms and hands, one holding a conch shell, one a discus, the third a club and the fourth a lotus. He is often shown sitting on a lotus flower with Lakshmi or reclining on the coils of the serpent, Shesha. His vehicle is Garuda, the mythical bird which is half-man and half-bird.

THE TEN AVATARS

Gods and demons are both active in the world and a constant struggle is being waged betwen the forces of good and evil. Usually the forces are well matched and a balance is maintained, but when the force of evil gains the upper hand and the balance is destroyed, Vishnu descends to earth in human or animal form as an incarnation, or *avatar*. The avatar always acts for a specific purpose.

Vishnu's first avatar was in the form of Matsya, the one-horned fish, through which the god predicted the deluge and towed the ship of the sage Vaivaswata to safety.

The second avatar was Kurma the tortoise, whose mission was to help recover some of the things that had been lost in the deluge. Gods and demons together set about churning the ocean of milk, using Mount Mandara as a churning stick. Vishnu, in the form of Kurma, lent his curved back for the mountain to rest on. Among the objects recovered were the precious *amrit*, or nectar of life; Lakshmi, or Sri, goddess of beauty and fortune and Vishnu's wife; Chandra, the moon, which Shiva took to wear on his piled-up hair; Surabhi, the cow of plenty; Airavata, a wonderful white elephant; and Rambha, a nymph, who became the first of the lovely *apsaras*, or celestial spirits.

The Themes

Vishnu's third incarnation was as Varaha the boar, for the destruction of the demon Hiranyaksha who, when asking for the boon of invulnerability from Brahma, recited the names of all the gods, demons, men and animals, but forgot the boar. When, misusing his powers, the demon dragged the world down to his own domain of dark waters, Vishnu took the form of the boar, as mighty as a lion and as big as a mountain, descended to the depths of the water, and killed the demon, recovering the *vedas* and releasing the earth so that it could float up to the water's surface again.

Vishnu then took the form of Narasinha, half-man half-lion, to defeat the demon, Hiranyakasipu. The brother of Hiranyaksha, he had Brahma's assurance that he would neither be killed by man, beast nor god, in the day or the night, inside or outside his house. Sure of immortality, he substituted the worship of the gods by worship of himself. However, his own son Prahlad, in spite of all persuasion and torture, remained an ardent devotee of Vishnu. In his rage the king tried to kill him by having him bitten by snakes, trampled by elephants, etc., but Prahlad could not be killed. Finally, one evening, the king pointed out a pillar in the doorway of his palace and demanded to know if Vishnu was there. Prahlad said he certainly was. At this, Vishnu, in the form of Narasinha, stepped out and tore Hiranyakasipu to pieces.

Vishnu's fifth incarnation as Vamana, strangely enough, was not against evil but against a good and honorable, but overambitious, king. Daitya Bali, Prahlad's grandson, was a well-loved ruler who governed wisely, but, having extended his dominion to the ends of the earth, found he could expand only in one direction— toward the realm of the gods. His power, gained by worship and sacrifices, could not be resisted, and the gods were turned out of their kingdom. It was decided that Vishnu should become incarnate as the son of Aditi and Kasyapa, one of the seven *rishis*, or sages. He grew up as the dwarf Vamana and approached the king to ask him for three paces of land. With the granting of the boon, Vishnu grew to enormous size and took two paces which covered heaven and earth. He desisted from taking the third step, and Bali was granted dominion over Patala, the nether regions, and was allowed to visit his lost domains once a year.

The sixth incarnation, Parasurama, took place to restore the power of the Brahmins against the Kshatriyas, the warriors. Vishnu came into the world as Parasurama, the youngest son of the Brahmin hermit Jamadagini. One day Jamadagini's wife was filled with impure thoughts which her husband divined. Incensed, he ordered his sons, as they returned from the forest, to kill their mother by striking off her head. They refused and their father cursed them and they became idiots. Parasurama, however, obeyed and cut off her head with Parasu, the axe given him by Shiva, after which he was named. The father was pleased with his obedience and offered him a boon. Parasurama then asked for the restoration of his mother's life and invincibility for himself in single combat. Both were granted to him.

Sometime later, a powerful Kshatriya king called Kartavirya, who had a thousand arms, was hunting in the forest and stopped at the hermit's home and took away the cow, Kamadhenu, which could fulfill all desires, despite the protests of Jamadagini's wife, who was alone at that time. Parasurama, hearing what happened, followed the king and killed him in single combat. Kartavirya's son, learning this, rushed to the hermitage and killed Jamadagini, who was alone. Parasurama vowed vengence on the whole Kshatriya clan and gradually exterminated all the menfolk. He then put the earth in the care of Kasyapa, father of the former avatar Vamana, and he himself retired into the mountains.

THE RAMAYANA

While Parasurama was still alive, Ramachandra, generally called Rama, the seventh avatar, appeared, and Parasurama became jealous of him. Their conflict forms part of the two epics, the *Ramayana* and the *Mahabharata*.

Rama appeared in order to quell Ravana, the ten-headed king of Lanka (Ceylon), the most dangerous and powerful demon king ever born. The story of this conflict is told in the *Ramayana*.

Ravana had practiced austerities and Brahma promised him immunity from death at the hands of gods and demons. Under cover of this immunity he began to persecute both men and gods. Since Ravana had been too proud to ask for immunity from men, Vishnu decided to take the form of a man, while the other gods lent their power to men and animals. He became all four sons of King Dasaratha. Rama was born to the king's first wife, Kaushalya, while another wife, Kaikeyi, gave birth to a son, Bharata, and Lakshmana and Satrughna were born to Sumitra. Rama, the oldest, inherited half Vishnu's nature, Bharata one-quarter, and the other two one-eighth each.

Rama and Lakshmana were particularly close. One day, hearing that Sita, the

The Themes

❦ 83 ❧

lovely daughter of King Janaka, was to be married, they went to the court, where the man who could bend a certain bow would be chosen as the bridegroom. Rama not only bent the bow but broke it, thus winning the girl's hand. Parasurama was annoyed with Rama for breaking the bow of Shiva and challenged him to a trial of strength. He was defeated and, consequently, excluded from a seat in the celestial world.

Soon after the marriage, King Dasaratha decided to abdicate in favor of his eldest son. But a maidservant of Queen Kaikeyi stirred up her feelings to make the king honor the boon he had promised long ago and place her son, Bharata, on the throne while Rama was exiled for fourteen years. Dasaratha was grief-stricken when Rama insisted on honoring the pledge and, accompanied by Sita and Lakshmana, left the city of Ayodhya to set out on his wanderings.

Bharata, who was away during this time, was furious when he heard this and went to the forest to urge Rama to return. On the latter's firm refusal he returned home and proceeded to reign as viceroy, placing Rama's sandals on the throne, a symbol that he was the rightful king.

In the forest Rama attracted the romantic attentions of Ravana's sister, Surpanakha. When her entreaties were rebuffed, she tried to attack Sita and swallow her, but Lakshmana cut off her nose, ears and breasts. Screaming, she rushed off and sent her younger brother, Khara, to revenge her. When Khara's vast army was destroyed, Surpanakha went to Ravana. She could arouse his interest only by dwelling on Sita's beauty and her fitness to be queen of Lanka.

Knowing the true identity of Rama, Ravana set about capturing Sita through a ruse. He sent an enchanted deer to the place where Sita usually spent her time. Sita was so enrapt by its beauty that she begged Rama and Lakshmana to capture it for her. During their absence Ravana abducted Sita in his aerial chariot and started for Lanka. On the way, Jatayu, king of the vultures, fought Ravana and was fatally wounded, but lived long enough to inform Rama, who was looking for Sita, of what had happened. Sita also implored the forests and rivers, over which she was flying, to inform Rama of her fate.

Having cremated Jatayu, Rama set about making plans to recover Sita. He made an alliance with the monkey king, Sugriva, and in return for a promise to help him recover his kingdom from which he had been exiled by his brother Bali, the king promised Rama support against Ravana. An army of monkeys and bears led by Hanuman, son of Vayu the wind, was raised and marched south.

Hanuman, who could fly, went ahead, and finding Sita alone in a garden in Ravana's palace, told her of the plans made for her deliverance. As he frolicked in the garden pulling up plants, Hanuman was caught and brought before Ravana. He saved his life by claiming diplomatic immunity—messengers from the enemy could not be killed—but Ravana ordered his tail to be set on fire. Hanuman ran around the city putting his blazing tail to good use and soon set fire to the whole of Lanka. He then returned to the mainland and gave Rama valuable information about the fortifications of Lanka. The city was built mostly of gold and was surrounded by seven moats and seven walls of stone and metal.

A bridge was constructed across the strait to Lanka and a mighty battle was fought before the gates of the city. Twice, Rama and Lakshmana were wounded but were saved by a herb brought by Hanuman all the way from the Himalayas. In spite of Kumbhakarana, Ravana's brother who swallowed hundreds of monkeys, the *rakshasa* (evil spirits) generals were all killed and the battle was settled by single combat between Rama and Ravana. The earth shook during the encounter; and as Rama cut off Ravana's head, another instantly grew in its place. Eventually, Rama drew the weapon given him by Agastya, a renowned sage, which flew straight to Ravana's chest, killing him, whereupon it returned to Rama. As Ravana died the gods rejoiced, raining flowers on Rama and raising the monkeys from the dead.

Sita returned to Rama, but he found it difficult to believe that she had preserved her virtue as Ravana's captive. To prove her innocence, Sita asked for the ordeal of fire, and as she threw herself on a burning pyre lit by Lakshmana, the sky proclaimed her innocence, and she was led by the fire god Agni to Rama, who accepted her.

On their return to Ayodhya, Rama was crowned king and the people rejoiced. However, the matter of Sita's chastity was still in doubt and, even though she was pregnant, Rama had to send her into exile. There, in the hermitage of the sage Valmiki, her twin sons Luv and Kush were born. Coming into the capital in their fifteenth year, the boys were recognized by their father, who then sent for Sita. In order that she should publicly declare her innocence, a large assembly was called and Sita asked the earth, her mother (for she was born of a furrow), to attest the truth of her words. The earth opened and took her back into its womb. Rama,

The Themes

now heartbroken, wished to follow her. He walked into the river Sarayu, where Brahma's voice welcomed him from heaven, and entered the glory of Vishnu.

The *Ramayana* is the oldest Sanskrit epic and was composed by Valmiki around the 5th century B.C. It gained popularity through the Hindi version of the poet Tulsidas (1532–1624). It is held in great esteem and regarded with veneration, and its many incidents have inspired all artists. Rama and Sita in exile are shown dressed in garments of leaves and Hanuman's agility and playfulness have made him a favorite with them. Indians may not know the *Ramayana* in detail, but they are conversant with the various incidents and are able to use them as examples for throwing light on current happenings. A verse in the introduction says, "He who reads and repeats this holy life-giving *Ramayana* is liberated from all his sins and exalted with all his descendants to the highest heaven."

THE KRISHNA LEGEND

Vishnu's eighth incarnation is as Krishna, who was incarnated for the destruction of his wicked uncle, King Kansa of Mathura. Krishna, by far the best loved of all the Hindu gods, inspires love and affection rather than reverence and awe. His childhood pranks—the stealing of butter and the upsetting of the pots of curds— and his amorous dalliances as a young man have been the subject of devotional songs for centuries and were responsible for perhaps the largest output of paintings in the country. The *bhakti* cult, of which he is the main inspiration, calls for love rather than severe austerities and endears Krishna to every Indian heart.

Bhakti implies devotion to God without any questioning. It is the path to salvation through love. Although the cult of Krishna is as old as Christianity, the *Bhagvata Purana*, dating from around the tenth century A.D., is the repository of the Krishna legend. The *Gita Govinda*, in praise of Krishna, composed in Bengal in the twelfth century by Jayadeva, is a collection of songs of the divine love of Radha and Krishna. The quality of the descriptive poetry, frankly erotic in parts, raised it to the realm of high art, its lyrical quality making it easy to memorize. The description of Krishna in this work provided the painter with guidelines which have always been faithfully followed: "His black body, sandal bedecked, clad in yellow, garlanded, with earrings dancing on his cheeks as he made sport."

The fifteenth and sixteenth centuries were the age of the great *bhakta*, or devotees, who spread the cult of Vishnu and his incarnations to all parts of India.

Indian Miniatures

Vallabha, the founder of the Vallabhacharya sect of Krishna worshipers, Surdas, the blind poet, Chaitanya, the saint, and Mira Bai, the poetess, were all devotees of Krishna.

It had been foretold that King Kansa of Mathura would be destroyed by a son born to his sister Devaki and her husband Vasudev. All their children were killed by order of the king, and when Krishna, their eighth son, was born, the father carried him secretly through a raging storm across the river Jamuna to the village of Gokul, where the boy was left by the side of the sleeping Yasoda, wife of Nand, chief herdsman of the village. Yasoda's daughter was taken away and substituted for Krishna. Miraculously, all knowledge of the substitution escaped the mind of Yasoda, and King Kansa, believing that his sister had given birth to a daughter, felt less uneasy.

Soon after, however, the king became anxious again and ordered the slaughter of every male child. He was helped in this task by demons who tried in various ways to take Krishna's life. The demoness Putana took the form of a beautiful woman and nursed Krishna at her poisoned breasts. Krishna sucked out her life substance so that she assumed the form of a whirlwind and lifted Krishna to the sky, but was herself dashed to destruction. Demons in the forms of a crane, a bull and an ass sought to destroy him, as did the serpent Kaliya, who lived in the Jamuna River and poisoned its water. Krishna defeated and killed them all except Kaliya, on whose many hoods he danced, assuming the weight of the whole world to crush the serpent. As the serpent began to die, however, his wife came to plead and beg for mercy, thus forcing Krishna to spare his life. The fight with Kaliya, which took place when Krishna was only a child, turned his skin blue, caused by the poison of the snake's fangs. The blue color, therefore, became a distinguishing mark of Krishna.

As a child Krishna's pranks were numerous. In Gokul he stole butter and upset the pots of curds. As a young man he went swimming with the milkmaids and stole the clothes of girls bathing in the river. He and his companions waylaid the maidens and demanded an embrace and a part of the curds they were carrying. If they refused, the pots would be upset and the scarves of the maidens snatched away. During the rainy season, he loved to swing ever higher with the girls, and during the festival of Holi he sprinkled them with color and got thoroughly sprinkled in turn. He participated in the everyday life of the village, tending the

The Themes

cattle, bringing them home in the evening and milking the cows, sometimes dressed as a milkmaid. He ate betel, played hide and seek and indulged in all kinds of flirtatious sport. The *gopis*, or milkmaids, loved him because he played the flute so beautifully, and for his lightheartedness and cheerful participation in life, came to treat him as one of themselves, and yet differently.

This apartness began when Krishna started to perform miracles. One day, Brahma, trying to assert his superiority over a fellow deity incarnate in the form of Krishna, spirited away the calves of a grazing herd in Gokul. When Krishna went to look for them, Brahma spirited away the cowherds, leaving them sleeping in a cave under a spell. Undaunted, Krishna created a similar herd and similar herdsmen, so that no one could tell the difference. After a year, Brahma found that the sleeping cowherds, or *gopas*, took on the likenesses of gods, while the ones created by Krishna went about their daily tasks. Realizing the greatness of Krishna, he asked his forgiveness and removed the spell. The herdsmen, not realizing the time that had passed, thanked Krishna for finding their calves so quickly and returned home happy.

In retaliation for Krishna having persuaded the inhabitants of the area to stop honoring him, Indra, the rain god, sent down torrents of rain which threatened to drown everything. Krishna lifted Govardhana, a hillock a few miles from Mathura, and held it up with his little finger, thus providing shelter for all the inhabitants.

He also opened his mouth and sucked in the flames of a raging fire that threatened to destroy the woods and kill all men and cattle.

Among his other acts of benevolence was his treatment of Sudama, a Brahmin, who had been his classmate. Sudama lived in poverty and, at a time of great need, was asked by his wife to go to Krishna for help. He went, taking with him a meager offering, which Krishna accepted. When Sudama returned home he found his hovel transformed into a palace.

In the course of time Krishna went to Mathura to take part in a tournament. There he defeated all of Kansa's wrestlers and slew the terrible elephant Kubaliya, which was sent to kill him. Then he killed Kansa and placed his own grandfather Ugrasena on the throne of Mathura.

Krishna left Mathura and went to Dwarka, where he married Rukmini, daughter of Raja Bhishmaka, after abducting her on the day of her wedding to another king who was an avatar of a demon. He married seven other women, each after a struggle with demons. When Nanaka, the powerful king of Pragjyotisha, became an implacable enemy of the gods and conquered them, Krishna captured 16,100 girls, both earthly and divine. After he had defeated Nanaka, Krishna married all the girls, for after seeing them he fell in love with each of them. He was able to delight them all simultaneously, and each bore him ten sons and one daughter.

Krishna was Arjuna's charioteer in the battle between the Pandavas and the Kauravas on the field of Kurukshetra, where he expounded his immortal *Gita*, the doctrine of karma, one of the fundamental creeds of Hinduism.

With the defeat of the Kauravas, a curse uttered by the mother of the deceased leader, Duryodhana, said that Krishna and all his people would perish. The people of Dwarka seemed to go mad for they killed each other leaving only Krishna, Balarama, his brother, who had been miraculously transferred from the womb of Devaki to that of another wife, Rohini, and the women. Balarama died and an arrow intended for a deer hit Krishna, who also died. Arjuna went to Dwarka to save the womenfolk by bringing them to Kurukshetra. On the way they were attacked by wild tribes who carried away most of the women.

All these episodes were depicted by the Rajput and Pahari painters. Some of them were used to illustrate the *Bhagvata Gita*, but many were painted for their own sake. To the story the painters, as earlier poets and writers had done, brought a mixture of devotion, rapture and mystic eroticism. Krishna remains a part of the community, but always above it. His waywardness remains inexplicable and incomprehensible as befits supreme beings. His flute symbolizes the call of the spirit to the human soul, and the women leaving everything to join Krishna symbolize the shedding of nonessentials in the pursuit of truth.

Since only metaphors within people's own experience are available to human beings, all metaphysical concepts have to be given a human or understandable form. The mystic aspect of the love for God thus is translated into the very physical terms of love between a man and woman. Being inspired by the divine, the miniature painter handled the love scenes with marked restraint. Even the most erotic scenes are imbued with spirituality and are free of any trace of vulgarity. They symbolize the yearning for the final union of the soul with God and thus the artists' handling of it is reverent. There are always a number of *gopis*, or milkmaids, but only one Krishna, and even though Radha is his main

The Themes

companion, she can never possess him to the exclusion of all others and must always share him. This is exemplified by the episode when the *gopis* thought they had conquered the heart of the Lord. To teach them a lesson, Krishna disappeared from their midst taking only Radha with him. The *gopis*, searching for Krishna, found Radha alone and sorrowing. She, having felt herself honored above the others, had endeavored to seal her triumph by asking him to carry her on his shoulders. At the moment of imagined victory, she found herself alone. Later, in response to the *gopis'* penitence, Krishna returned and danced with them. Flowers rained down and celestial drums sounded, and Krishna stood in the center while the *gopis* sang and danced around him. Soon, however, a Krishna appeared between every pair of *gopis*, giving each the cherished illusion of having danced individually with the God.

In the course of his discourse on the meaning of life at the battle of Kurukshetra, Krishna dwells on the interchangeability of matter and energy. Nothing, he says, is either born or dies. All stems from one source and returns to the same source. Pictorially, this is one of the most beautiful depictions of Krishna, where he is shown as supreme without beginning or end, with all creation entering him and flowing out of him.

The Krishna legend became the most beloved of all the painting themes, especially as it allowed the artist unlimited opportunity to exercise his ingenuity. Few themes offer the same blending in of worship and lighthearted frolic, and the Indian painter has made the most of his opportunity. Krishna appears at all ages and in all moods, while Radha is shown in all possible *nayika* (heroine) moods. The pictures of his childhood days and his youth are gay and suffused with a lightness of spirit. Even in certain more serious episodes, the tone is always imbued with sparkle and optimism. The pastoral setting for these early days provides endless opportunities for the artist to display his knowledge of the quirks of human nature and the incidents of day-to-day living. In all schools, the later episodes, like the abduction of Rukmini, are treated with a lack of enthusiasm, without the ebullience of the earlier paintings, as if the artist found the task not entirely to his liking.

The ninth incarnation of Vishnu was the Buddha. As such the Buddha is not the straightforward upholder of righteousness, but a propagator of ideas which would lead to wickedness and thus weaken the opponents of the gods and cause them either to be destroyed or to turn to the old faith for salvation. This allowed the main figure of a dissident movement to be absorbed into the Hindu pantheon.

The tenth or last incarnation, Kalki, is yet to come. It will usher in the end of the present age and all values will deteriorate, and only outward show and pure materialism will remain. Truth and love will disappear and physical love will be the sole bond between man and woman. When all signs of civilization pass away, leaving man wearing the bark of trees and eating wild fruits, Vishnu will appear on earth riding a white horse, Kalki. The blazing sword in Vishnu's hand will destroy the wicked, thus preparing the world for the renewal of creation and the resurgence of virtue in the next cycle of existence.

The Goddesses of Mythology

The goddesses in Hindu mythology embody certain qualities and moods, such as beauty, wisdom, extreme ferocity and also destructive tendencies. The following are the most frequently depicted goddesses.

Lakshmi: the consort of Vishnu, also known as Sri. She is generally represented sitting or standing on a lotus. A beautiful, golden woman with two or four arms, she is the goddess of fortune and the giver of wealth.

Saraswati: the consort of Brahma and the goddess of music, poetry and the creative arts, learning and science. She is represented as a beautiful, light-skinned woman carrying a musical instrument.

Devi: the consort of Shiva, the most powerful and complex of goddesses. She is *sakti*, female energy, and as Parvati, Sati, Durga and Kali, she embodies both the benign and fierce aspects of human nature. She is light and beauty, the symbol of fertility but also that of ferocity. In her malignant form, Devi is known as Durga, represented as a beautiful woman with a hostile expression. She rides a tiger and has either four or ten arms. When depicted killing the demon Durga, from whom she takes her name, strength and menace radiate from her.

Even more terrifying than Durga is Kali, who is associated with the darkest aspects of human nature—killing and witchcraft. She has black skin, teeth like tusks, a protruding tongue dripping with blood and a blood-smeared face with a third eye in the center of the forehead. In two of her four arms she holds a weapon

The Themes

and a severed head dripping blood, while the other two are raised to bless worshipers. Her body is bare except for some gruesome ornaments, such as necklaces of skulls and serpents, earrings made of little children and a girdle from which hang the hands of demons.

Other aspects of Kali are Chandi the Fierce and Bhairavi the Terrible. The latter is the counterpart of Shiva as Bhairava, who destroys for the pleasure he derives from this.

The Animals of Mythology

Animals have a special place in Indian life since reincarnation, the cycle of life, may bring a person to earth in any form. This explains the emphasis on the doctrine of *karma*—do your duty well so that you will not be born into a lower form of life. Even though the animal state is considered lower than the human state, the very fact that one can be born into either one makes for a strong sense of kinship. This has been further fostered by the idea of the divinity and power of certain species. Thus, monkeys, reflecting the form of Hanuman, hold a special niche in Indian culture as does the snake, whose reign over the secret areas of earth and water is undisputed.

Some of the best products of the Mughal ateliers are paintings of birds and animals. The realistic treatment of human beings is also extended to animals, and they are portrayed with an amazing range of expression and character. In Rajput and Pahari paintings, birds and animals are introduced for their mystical significance and to emphasize a mood. Elephants, the symbol of grandeur and greatness, are the only animals that are painted alone, and even when shown accompanied by their mahouts, they are the central figures on the canvas. Thus, elephants fighting, running amok or enjoying a lovely bath on a steaming hot day are found in large numbers in Rajput miniatures.

The religious aspect of animals has not escaped the attention of the painters, and animal deities are painted with love and reverence and with great attention to individual characteristics. The following are the best-known animal deities.

GANESH

A short, potbellied man with four arms and an elephant's head, he is one of the most popular of Hindu deities and is considered to be the bringer of good luck and the remover of all obstacles. He is the god of wisdom and prudence, a good scribe and learned in the scriptures: it was he who wrote the scriptures, at the dictation of the sage Vyasa. He is propitiated at the beginning of any venture, journey or business deal.

Explanations of the origin of his elephant's head vary. One version relates that Shiva was in the habit of surprising Parvati at her bath. She disliked this habit and thought of a way to discourage it. Scraping the scurf from her body, she mixed it with oil and ointments and formed it into a man's body. She gave it life by sprinkling it with water from the Ganges. She put the figure outside to guard her bathroom door. Shiva, trying to enter, was incensed that his way was barred and cut off Ganesh's head. Parvati was overcome with grief and, to comfort her, Shiva sent out messengers to bring him the head of the first creature they saw. This happened to be an elephant, and its head was planted on Ganesh's shoulders. In another version Ganesh is the son of Shiva and Parvati.

Still another version has it that so many people obtained access to heaven by visiting the shrine of Somnath that heaven was filled to overflowing while hell was empty. The gods approached Parvati, who rubbed her body and produced a being, Ganesh, who could induce in men a desire for riches so strong they would never think of spending time in making pilgrimages.

In spite of his potbelly and enormous head, Ganesh is always depicted as dignified and even graceful. Some representations of him dancing make him appear very light on his feet and able to carry his bulk well.

GAJENDRA MOKSA

This aquatic monster seized the king of the elephants as he was drinking at a pool. As the elephant was being dragged under water, it prayed to Vishnu for help, raising a lotus in its trunk as an offering. Vishnu, riding on Garuda, killed the monster and freed the elephant. This is a subject often met with in Rajput and Pahari painting.

GARUDA

He is the king of the birds who is swifter than the wind. He has the head, wings, talons and beak of an eagle, and the body and limbs of a man. He roams about the

The Themes

world devouring evil men and has an unrelenting hatred for snakes. He is the son of the sage Kasyapa and Vinita, the daughter of Daksha (Brahma's son born from his thumb), being hatched from an egg laid by her. He is Vishnu's mount.

HANUMAN

This monkey god is renowned for his learning, agility and speed, and for his loyalty to Rama. He was born to the monkey queen Anjana, as one of the creatures fathered by the gods who could assist Rama in the destruction of Ravana. When this aim was fulfilled, Rama offered Hanuman any boon he cared to name. Hanuman asked to be allowed to live for as long as men spoke of Rama, thus acquiring immortality, for the memory of Rama will never die.

THE NAGAS

This race of serpents are the sons of Kasyapa and his principal wife, Kadru. They are the guardians and powerful rulers of the nether regions, Patala. They have five or seven hoods, and their jewels, the best of the three worlds, light up the nether regions.

The women *nagas* are slight and lovely. Though most of the *nagas* are considered evil, some of them have been touched by divinity through their connection with the gods. Shesha, king of the *nagas*, is the constant companion of Vishnu and forms the raft on which the god lies floating on the cosmic waters at the dawn of creation. He is also known as Ananta and, with his tail in his mouth, is the symbol of eternity.

OTHER RELIGIOUS THEMES

JAINISM

To the Jains, time is an eternally revolving wheel with six periods of degeneration and six of progessive improvement. Each of these produce twenty-four Tirthankaras, "one who has escaped from the wheel of life," one of whom was Mahavira. The Tirthankaras have value as objects of meditation, although they cannot intercede for the faithful because there is no ultimate God. Many of the Tirthankaras seem to have connections with Hindu mythology. Of the Tirthankaras of the present age, for instance, the first, Rishabadeva, attained nirvana on Mount Kailash, the abode of Shiva; the eleventh was born of parents who were both called Vishnu; and the twenty-second, Neminatha, was born in Dwarka and was a cousin of Krishna.

Mahavira lived around the same time as Buddha, i.e., in the fifth century B.C. His parents were already Jains. Before his birth his mother, Trisala, had a series of sixteen dreams which foretold the greatness of her coming son. She saw a white elephant, a white bull, a white lion, Lakshmi, fragrant *mandara* flowers, the radiant moon, the sun, a jumping fish, a golden pitcher, a lake filled with lotus flowers, an ocean of milk, a celestial palace, a vase as high as the mythological Mount Meru filled with gems, a fire fed by sacrificial butter, a ruby and diamond throne, and a celestial king ruling on earth. The child was transferred into her womb from that of a Brahmin's wife. He was of exceptional beauty and had great physical and spiritual strength. His name was Vardhamana. He obtained Enlightenment under an *asoka* tree watched by the gods, who lifted and carried him to a park, set him on a five-tiered throne and acknowledged him as Mahavira. He tore off his clothes and shaved his hair. (The Digambara sect believes that Mahavira wore no clothes after that, while the Svetambara sect believes that he wore a white robe presented him by Indra.)

He was totally indifferent to his surroundings and was impervious to pain. Whether people tried to steal the clothes on his body, drive nails into his ears or scorch his feet, he sat still, deep in meditation, oblivious to what was happening to his physical self.

Just before his death, he spent seven days preaching to all the rulers of the earth, enjoining them above all not to kill—not only humans but animals, birds, insects, in fact, any living thing. This led to the belief that the most virtuous life is spent sitting and fasting. His death took place unseen by his followers, who fell asleep, waking to find the world plunged in darkness. Mahavira became a *siddha*, "a soul of greatest perfection," freed from the cycle of rebirth and detached from karma.

The Jain scriptures, which recount the history of the Tirthankaras, contain some of the earliest extant examples of Indian painting.

BUDDHISM

Mahamaya, wife of King Suddhodana of Kapilavastu, dreamt one night of a white elephant entering her womb. She became pregnant, and gave birth from

The Themes

her side while standing beneath a *sal* tree, The child was born fully developed and took seven steps to the north. Astrologers predicted that the boy, Siddharta, would either be the greatest king or the greatest ascetic the world has ever seen.

He was carefully educated to be a king and was shielded from all exposure to the outside world. He was to marry Yasodhara, a lovely young princess, who had been his wife in previous lives and had promised to be his wife in all incarnations.

The young couple led an idyllic life, full of pleasure and happiness. But Siddharta was restless and had an urgent desire to see something of the world outside the palace and begged his father to let him go out. Suddhodana had the streets cleared and ordered that no old or infirm person should be present along the route the prince was to take. Yet on his very first outing, Siddharta saw an old man. He was astonished to see this figure and even more so when Chandaka, his charioteer, explained that all men are subject to old age. On other occasions, he saw a dead man carried on a bier, a sick and helpless man and a monk who was calm and controlled. He thus learnt that all those born must die, that sickness comes to all, and that only through renunciation can one find peace for oneself and for others. Leaving his wife and infant son sleeping one night, he left the palace with his charioteer never to return.

Siddharta got rid of his jewels and cut off his hair, which he gave to the charioteer to take back to Kapilavastu. He then set off on his journey in search of the Truth and joined the pupils of the great sages, Kalama and Rudraka, but even on completion of his studies he still felt dissatisfied. He practiced severe austerities, but decided that asceticism was no more the path to Enlightenment than knowledge. He sat down under a pipal tree, determined not to rise until he had achieved Enlightenment.

The chief of the evil spirits, Mara, tried to interrupt his meditations by hurling stones, javelins, rocks and burning charcoal on him, but Siddharta took no notice. Then the demon sent his three lovely daughters to tempt him, but still he remained unmoved. After four times seven days of fasting and meditation, he obtained Enlightenment and became the Buddha, the "Enlightened One."

He preached the doctrine of the four Holy Truths—that birth, age, sickness and death are sorrow, as is the clinging to material things, that the chain of reincarnation is the direct result of attachment to life and desire, that the extinction of desire is essential for detachment, and that the only way to extinguish desires is to follow the Eightfold Path. This consists of the right belief, right intention, right words, truth and openness, right conduct, right living, right effort toward self-control, right thinking—applying the mind to religious experience—and right meditation on all the mysteries of life.

The success of Buddha's teachings created many enemies. Devadatta, his cousin, who had been a childhood rival, failed in his attempts both to create a schism among the Buddha's followers and to kill him. Devadatta's failure to harm the Great One made his own followers convert to the new creed.

When the Buddha felt death approaching, he went to a grove of *sal* trees which were flowering out of season and lay down for his last rest on earth. When his soul left his body, the wind howled and light vanished from the earth, while the heavens were lit up by a strange light and flashes of lightning.

As the concept of Buddhism became more developed, it incorporated many features of Hinduism. The goddesses of the Buddhist pantheon are reminiscent of Durga and Kali—Tara, who is yellow, red or blue when she threatens, and white or green when she is gentle and loving, is the most revered of all. The *Jatakas*, accounts of the Buddha's previous lives, show that he acquired great strength and moral stature with each successive incarnation, until he finally reached his full stature as the Buddha.

Unfortunately, examples of paintings of the period of Buddhist domination in India are very limited and only found in mural form. Very few examples on palm leaf exist. However, it is the Buddhist paintings in the caves of Ajanta and Ellora that give us the earliest references to Indian painting.

TANTRA AND YANTRA

Popularly, Tantra is associated with magic and secret, rather fearsome rituals performed on dark nights in deserted places. A Tantrist is one who worships Devi, the most powerful of all goddessess, not in the general way in which she is worshiped all over India, but in a secret form which, if properly handled, takes the practitioner forward in his quest of spiritual awakening and self-realization. Devi, or *sakti* (power), cannot be worshiped alone, and whatever her form, is always paired with her male counterpart Bhairava-Shiva. Worship is through the chanting of *mantra*, combinations of sounds charged with deep meaning. Repeated chanting awakens the dormant centers of energy in the body. To the

The Themes

Tantrist who has advanced on the way to self-realization, the effort is toward visualization of the flow of cosmic currents from the Supreme Energy (Brahma) to the point when the idea of creation takes shape in the divine mind. It is as if one was present at the great drama of the beginning of creation.

Tantra art is firmly rooted in spiritual values, and for the Tantra artist it is a continuous process of the discovery of the roots of the universe which he has discovered within himself and which he must make available for others as a medium for the discovery of the past, present and future, all at one time. Art is not a profession, but a path toward truth and self-realization.

Yantra is essentially a geometrical composition, but in reality it is a revealed image of an aspect of cosmic structure. The Yantras are composed of lines, rectangles; squares and other geometrical forms, each visible form carrying with it its own implicit power pattern. All experience can be harmonized within the individual by yoking the opposites present in him. The interlocking triangles of Yantra represent the male and female principles, without which no movement, or creation, can take place.

The spheroid stands for the world egg, the duality of *purusha* (person) and *prakriti* (nature). In Tantric painting, this division is indicated by red and white colors, red symbolizing the female, and white the male essence. The *bindu* or "point" is the central focus of Yantra. It has existence but no magnitude, and carries within itself the seeds of its future, this being symbolically represented in painting by white and red points. It is the ultimate point, beyond which a thing or energy cannot be condensed, and is the nucleus both of matter and of radiant consciousness. *Kundalini sakti*, "coiled and dormant cosmic power," present in every human body, when awakened, finds passage through the spinal cord to the point at the junction of the eyebrows. At this point, the self is shed and union with the Absolute achieved. This is the ultimate goal of all Tantrists.

The Tantric artist delights in showing the movement of the roused *kundalini*, or energy, the forms of the *bindu* in ascent or descent, in colors which have a definite significance. The role of woman as wife, mother and temptress, so freely depicted in India, can also be considered Tantric, since all are varying manifestations of Devi.

❧ *4* ❧

The Schools

PALA

The earliest extant miniature paintings are those that were done on palm leaf in eastern and western India in the eleventh and twelfth centuries A.D. Those in the eastern region of Bihar and Bengal were done under the patronage of the kings of the Pala dynasty (seventh to twelfth centuries A.D.). As the kings were patrons of Buddhism, the paintings had for their subject stories from the *Jatakas* and other Buddhist subjects. It is interesting to note their similarity to the frescoes at Ajanta. The fact that both had their inspiration in Buddhism can hardly be sufficient to explain the similarity of styles of two regions set geographically so far apart.

The square lower lip, the long, narrow slanting eyes and strongly arched brows are almost identical in both places. But the most striking feature is the similarity of pose. The inclined head and the curve of the body in both schools could have been done by the same hand. It is possible that as the output of this school was very small, no attempt was made at innovation and the earlier established style was continued with very slight local variations.

The hierarchical concept of Indian art is extremely prominent in Pala painting: the main figure dwarfs all the others. The symbolism of color is also apparent. The central figures are green, symbol of rain and fertility, while the background is red, denoting sensuousness and passion. It is almost as if the subject has emerged from the realm of worldly desires into a sphere of peace, calm and fruitfulness.

JAIN

Nothing could be more different from the Ajanta style of painting than that which developed in western India and was used to illustrate the religious manuscripts of the Jains. Why the Jain painters, when they were geographically much closer to Ajanta, evolved such a violently different style, cannot even partially be explained in terms of different beliefs, for Jainism, like Buddhism, has as its basic creed an abhorrence of killing and, therefore, of violence. There is, however, in these miniatures a vital rhythm of movement and an angularity of line that denotes action rather than pure thought.

The Jain miniatures were produced in great numbers. The copying and illustration of religious manuscripts won merit for the man who commissioned the work, and vast quantities of manuscripts were, therefore, written and illustrated in Gujarat and Rajasthan, where the Jain community flourished. Kings who ruled this area between the tenth and thirteenth centuries built temples and established libraries which contained thousands of manuscripts. The sumptuousness of the work executed depended on the financial status of the man commissioning it, and it can be presumed that those which were written in gold were not meant for reading but as objects of veneration, reflecting the wealth of the patron. Jain temples throughout the country even today are rich repositories of such literature.

The main characteristic of Jain painting is the protruding further eye when there is a two-thirds view of the face. This could have been a device used to give the sense of a third dimension and to redeem the picture from flatness. This great emphasis on the eyes is also a characteristic of Jain sculpture, specially that found in temples of the Svetambara sect. In metal sculpture the eye is painted white and, in both metal and stone, glass eyes are frequently set in over the carving. This is usually so only in statues of saviors and monks and may be attributed to the special place given to the eye in Indian thought. It is the window of the soul and a powerful means of projecting one's own power into the world and influencing people. In the plastic arts, obviously, it is possible to convey this only through a special device.

In his art, however, the painter gives the same eye to all his subjects, endowing them with an air of fierce alertness. The long nose ending in a sharp point at the tip enhances the fierceness in appearance. This, in turn, is subtly subdued by the hint of a double chin, softly rounded arms and curved surfaces. The chin itself is sharp and pointed.

Male figures are somewhat lion-shaped, with rounded chest and tapering waists. The head is disproportionately large, giving the body a foreshortened look. In early Jain art male figures are hardly distinguishable from female figures. The fact that women wear a dot on the forehead while men wear a V-shaped mark is not always valid, for quite often kings and monks also wear the dot. Monks and nuns, however, can be distinguished by their clothes. The nun's robe covers the whole body and extends beyond the neck, while the monk's robe stops at the neck, leaving one shoulder bare.

The use of halos is a common Jain characteristic. The nimbus, supposed to have originated in ancient Persia, traveled to Byzantium and came back to Persia and India. At moments of joy and celebration the Jain halo is ornamented; otherwise it is left plain.

The drawing in early pictures is executed in black outline, and the colors used are vivid yellows, crimson, green and black, with some blue. Red and black backgrounds are common. The painting was done only after the text was completed. Most often the illustrations were completed along with the text, but sometimes they remained unpainted so that the text was followed by a blank space. The different registers in a Jain miniature denote the continuation of a story or two separate incidents.

Palm leaf was used till the fourteenth century, when paper came into vogue. The leaves were threaded with cotton and enclosed within wooden covers, the insides of which were also painted. The pages were, of necessity, long and narrow, and the design was impressed into the leaves with a stylus and the impression made filled in with ink or charcoal dust. The use of paper broadened the artist's scope and gave him more space to work on. The palm leaf format, however, persisted, and the pages continued to be long and narrow, although much broader than the earlier palm leaf pages. Thus the dimensions changed from 22 in. by 2 1/2 in. to 12 in. by 4 in.

Borders were ornamented with pictures of elephants, swans and flowers. The love of the sumptuous displayed itself in the lavish use of gold and ultramarine, carmine and green. Faces, especially of the women, became better finished and

The Schools

the drawing lost its extreme angularity of line and became smoother. Animals and birds were more natural and less stylized.

Apart from religious painting, the fifteenth-century painting of Gujarat shows themes that are purely secular, with frankly erotic and romantic love scenes. Incidents from the life of Krishna are also found.

The greater movement of people and commodities between India and the Middle East inevitably resulted in some pervasive foreign influence. Illustrations in the *Kalpasutras*, the Jain holy scriptures, show foreigners wearing their own native dress.

Jain traders carried their art wherever they went and as a result paintings showing strong Jain influences were made in places like Jaunpur in north India, Malwa in central India and Orissa in the east.

MALWA

Malwa was subdued by the Delhi sultans in the fourteenth century. In 1401 Dilawar Khan Ghori, who had been appointed governor of Malwa by the king of Delhi, assumed royal status. In 1428, Malwa was invaded by the Bahmani king Ahmad Shah, but the result of the battle was indecisive. There were frequent conflicts with Mewar, which was forced to accept Malwa suzerainty in 1454. Gradually the surrounding areas including Bundi, Kotah and Ranthambor were occupied, and Malwa became the dominant power in the region.

The court of Malwa, located at Mandu in central India, provided great patronage of the arts. Being Muslims, the rulers obviously had strong ties with Central Asia, where the development of painting had connections with both China and Arabia. (This will be dealt with at length in the section on Mughal painting.) During the fifteenth century contact with Persia was established, and painters, calligraphers and manuscripts arrived in great numbers at the Indian court. Persian works such as *Bustan*, the poetic tales of the thirteenth-century poet Saadi, were written and illustrated. *Nimatnamah*, or "The Book of Delicacies" (a cookery book), was written and illustrated around 1500, and shows a distinct mingling of the Shiraz style with that reminiscent of the Jain, although less stylized. The Mongol features of some of the courtiers, the Persian clothes of some of the women and the formalized vegetation are combined with distinctly Indian features, such as the squatting posture of the cook, the shape of the cooking vessels, and the facial features and draperies of some of the women. The generally relaxed atmosphere in the paintings is quite different from the highly formalized style of Persian painting of the period.

By 1540, when *Laur Chanda*, a romantic poem, came to be illustrated, Indian elements became dominant, although the Persian background still existed. Jain elements persisted in the draperies and a slight air of fierce vitality in the work. However, the protruding eye is completely absent, as it was in the *Nimatnamah*, and the open Indian admiration of the female form, so different from the Persian treatment where women are decorously covered up, becomes more obvious.

The love of the ruler Baz Bahadur for the courtesan Rupmati is a favorite subject of the Malwa artist. Although the romance came to a sad end with the defeat of Baz Bahadur by the Mughals in 1561 and the suicide of Rupmati, its ardor and intensity caught the imagination of poets and painters long after the subjects had passed away. An ardent musician and poet, Baz Bahadur composed in Persian, Avadhi and Hindi, and brought about a fusion of Hindu and Muslim cultures. The depiction of *raga* and *ragini* was started in earnest around this time.

Malwa women have sturdy, well-formed bodies, with arms tapering to very fine wrists, at the ends of which are strong, capable hands. The forehead, a continuation of the nose, is broad and low, and rises to meet a flat crown. The eyes are long and wide open, and even when the nose is slightly tilted up to give an air of piquancy, it detracts little from the general air of resolute purposefulness. The hair is braided into a long plait which hangs down stiffly to the hips and is often tied at the end with ornamental tassels. A filmy scarf covers the head, revealing a number of hair ornaments. The sash hangs low down the front, flaring out stiffly at the ends. Figures are usually projected against a background of solid color.

The colors of the earlier paintings are primary—reds, greens, blues, with touches of pink and yellow, but later colors fade to pastels with a lavish use of gold.

Trees are stylized with abundant foliage, and even banana plants are depicted with foliage overflowing in fixed patterns.

ORISSA

As has been stated earlier, the Jains carried their art with them wherever they went, and Orissa, on the east coast, shows the Jain influence in the same way as Malwa. In fact, there is a striking resemblance between Orissa and Malwa painting, and except for some outstanding differences, one could easily be mistaken for the other.

The Orissa artist loved ornamentation and every available inch of space is decorated, with the possible exception of the patches of color against which the human figures are projected. Leafy trees with sinuous trunks are a feature of this area. Outlines are ornamented with bands of color or rows of dots, which are often doubled for greater effect.

As painting developed, so did the ornamentation, until the whole background and the clothes came to be scattered with flowers and the sky with stars. Eyes are wide open, with the whites emphasized for greater effect. Fingernails and toenails are sharply delineated and the women's nose rings stand out stiffly. Colors are vibrant, and swarms of bees and highly decorated clothing with stiff draperies give Orissa painting its special flavor. There is a surging vital quality to the whole which later deteriorated, and the pictures lost their vitality to become static and purely ornamental.

The cultural climate which fostered the erotic sculptures of the famous temple of Konarak in Orissa was obviously pervasive when the paintings were done, and illustrations to the *Kamasutra*, the Indian treatise on love, along with incidents from the story of Radha and Krishna, were the main themes of the Orissa painter.

The use of palm leaf continued in Orissa until the nineteenth century, long after it had gone out of use everywhere else. The manuscripts were written and illustrated in the same way as the Jain manuscripts, but the pictures were not always colored. Black and white drawings were quite common and, even in the colored drawings, the colors used were always subtle.

MUGHAL

Islam originated in Arabia and had no art of its own, but its followers, spreading to other countries, assimilated the art and culture of the conquered peoples and made them their own. In spite of the fact that Islamic doctrine forbids representations of the human face or form, Muslims have produced some of the finest paintings representing man in his worldly preoccupations that the world has ever seen.

Indian Miniatures

Muslim kings, while destroying the religious art of those not mentioned as "people of the Book," drew talent from the various flourishing centers of arts and crafts to their own courts. They offered artists generous patronage so they could devote their time fully to the pursuit of their art without having to think of the problems of day-to-day living. The Sassanid empire of Persia of the fourth to seventh centuries A.D. was one of the most powerful in the world when the Muslims descended on it, destroying all vestiges of its artistic achievement and converting the population to Islam. At the eastern end of this empire lay the great overland route connecting the Far East with the rest of the known world. This route was the center of ecclesiastical architecture crossfertilized by the various influences of India, China, Greece and the Christian countries.

The Arab cities that grew up in Mesopotamia vied in grandeur with the cities of the Persian subjects that had been destroyed. An amalgam of nationalism and stiff formalism flavored the painting of this area in the thirteenth century. That commerce with India was well established is evidenced in the brown-skinned Indian figures in cotton clothes that appear in these paintings, just as the Middle Eastern figures in long gowns appear in Jain miniatures.

This rather tentative Arab art was, in turn, swept away by the Mongols, the Central Asian nomadic people who descended on the Middle East like a host of locusts and destroyed Baghdad in 1258. Their aesthetic inspiration obviously came from China, which was very highly developed in the arts. Chinese craftsmen were brought over to embellish palaces and to illustrate books. Later, craftsmen from Persia were sent to China so that Persia acquired a good deal of Chinese art, while Chinese painting and porcelain came to be decorated with the Kufic script. The artists tried to meet the requirements of their patrons but could not keep the local element entirely out of their work. Thus, though fourteenth-century Persian painting is strongly Chinese in character, it is also undoubtedly Persian.

At this period painting probably developed in Azerbaijan or Tabriz, where the court assembled. Later it developed further east at Samarkand and Bokhara on the Oxus, where Timur, popularly known in the West as Tamerlane, ruled. A terror to his enemies, his concern for the arts and learning was notable. His patronage of the arts was inherited by his sons, and Shah Rukh, his favorite son, sent an embassy to China which included the renowned artist, Ghiyasud-din Khalil, who was instructed to record everything he saw.

The Schools

How far the art, especially of portraiture, was developed at this time is narrated by Ibn Batuta, an Arab traveler who was in China in 1347. "On one occasion that I visited the emperor's own city and the imperial palace with my companions, I passed through the bazaar of the painters. In the evening, on leaving the palace, I passed again through the same bazaar, and there I saw my own portrait and that of my companions painted on sheets of paper and hung on the walls. We all stopped to examine the likeness and everybody found that of his neighbor to be excellent; I was told that the emperor had ordered the painters to make our likenesses, and that they had come to the palace for this purpose whilst we were there. They studied us and painted us without our knowing anything of the matter. In fact, it is an established custom among the Chinese to make the portrait of every visitor to the country."

The most brilliant work under the descendants of Shah Rukh was done in Khorasan toward the end of the fifteenth century. Here gathered a galaxy of poets, writers, historians and painters, among them the great Bihzad, whose special gift was portraiture and whose influence on the art of the period was extremely widespread. He made faces more realistic, compared with their previous impersonality in which only a beard or mustache distinguished a male from a female. Each face now acquired character, giving the person it portrayed a distinct individuality. After the death of Sultan Hussain Mirza, whom he had served for thirty years, he joined the service of Shah Ismail, founder of the Saffavid dynasty of Persia.

Sufism, the mystical branch of Islam dedicated to the elimination of self and to union with God, was at this time flourishing in Persia. It made its tenets known through poetry, which used the analogies of human love and drunkenness to express the striving of the soul toward its creator and the state of ecstasy. Interestingly enough, the same concepts and analogies—except for drinking—are the distinguishing features of the *bhakti* cult, which in India became inextricably linked with the Krishna legend.

The second ruler of the dynasty, Shah Tahmasp I, continued patronage of the arts, and considerable work was done at Tabriz, Herat and Shiraz. The mystic overtones of the paintings of the earlier period now disappeared, and young men reclining under blossoming trees, drinking and feasting scenes, lovers writing poems to the beloved or gazing at their portraits peopled the canvases of the time. The work was very painstakingly executed with minute brushstrokes and fine calligraphy. Faces are Mongol, round with narrow eyes and extremely high cheekbones. A wealth of stylized flora and fauna adorns the works.

Babar (1483–1530), the first Mughal emperor of India, was a descendant of Timur through his mother, who was called "Mughal"—probably a corruption of the word "Mongol"—a title which gave the dynasty its name. His autobiography, which he found time to write during his innumerable campaigns, is one of the finest Indian literary works ever produced. His one recorded remark on painting gives an idea of his critical faculty. The great Persian artist Bihzad, he says, "was a very elegant painter, but he did not draw young, beardless faces well. He made the neck too large. Bearded faces he painted extremely well."

Babar became emperor in 1526 and ruled for four years. His son, Humayun, was ousted from the throne and spent fifteen years in exile. One of these years, 1544, the most memorable in terms of Indian painting, was spent at the court of Shah Tahmasp of Persia. The love of the arts was in Humayun's blood and he was quite dazzled by the artistic output of the Persian court. He met two distinguished pupils of Bihzad, Khwaja Abdus Samad and Mir Saiyyid Ali, and invited them to India when he regained his throne for only seven months in 1555. It was from these artists that Humayun and his son, Akbar, took lessons in drawing. An atelier was set up in the palace and the serious work of painting began.

The two Persian artists were the guiding spirits for the *Dastan-i-Amir Hamza*, the first of the great series of paintings which gave the Mughal school its name and reputation. This was produced in the reign of Humayun's son, Akbar (1556–1605). The majority of painters in the atelier were Indians who had been trained in the existing school of painting in India. Even though the masters guided these apprentices to produce works using purely Persian techniques, their basic Indian training soon asserted itself and a synthesis of the two styles emerged in their works, producing a school of painting which has been the subject of unlimited praise by all critics and connoisseurs.

The artists worked together on a sort of assembly line basis, where each developed his own specialty—the first outline sketch, the filling in of color, landscape or facial features. When the picture was finished, the superintendent would write the names of all the painters responsible on it, so the earliest Mughal paintings were far from being anonymous.

The Schools

The term "Imperial Mughal" denotes the work done under four emperors: Akbar (1556–1605); Jahangir (1605–27); Shah Jahan (1628–58); and Aurangzeb (1658–1707). This period also embodied the beginning, rise and decline of Mughal painting.

Akbar himself, surprisingly enough, could neither read nor write. How this was possible in a man of superb intellect can only be explained by the fact that quite early in life he had consciously blocked out all book learning. He took knowledge in through the ears and had someone read to him from his enormous library, which after his death was calculated to be worth 700,000 pounds sterling. He had books translated from Arabic, Sanskrit and other languages into Persian for his use, and he had his own actions and the details of his administration set down in the *Akbarnamah*, written by his friend and courtier, Abul Fazl. Orders were also given to the older members of the community who had firsthand experience of great events to record their memoirs.

Akbar's Muslim faith was not extreme and he ignored the Prophet's strong injunction against the representation of the human figure, basically calculated to prevent idolatry and to keep man from copying God's handiwork, although this had been, as we have seen, ignored by the even more devout Muslims. While the really orthodox believers contented themselves with calligraphy and abstract design for decorative purposes, Akbar defended the painter by saying that he had special opportunities for the recognition of God, for the exercise of his art teaches him humility. Even though he can draw the perfect likeness of a human being, he knows that his work must remain without life and so his thoughts turn to God, the giver of life. Akbar had various works illustrated.

The *Dastan-i-Amir Hamza*, a massive work comprising 1,400 paintings, took fifteen years to complete. It tells of the exploits of the uncle of the prophet Mohammed, Amir Hamza, while spreading the Muslim faith, and was painted in a series of exceptionally large-sized pictures—22 inches by 28 1/2 inches on cotton cloth. The canvases teem with life, recounting episodes in which Amir Hamza battles against various enemies and evil spirits to complete his mission. The sharp brushstrokes, lush vegetation and swirling waters give a sense of urgency to the whole. The Persian flavor is extremely strong, but Indian elements are evident in the shape of faces or the vitality and majesty of an elephant.

Other works that were illustrated in Akbar's reign included the *Khamsa* of Nizami, a classic of Persian literature; the romantic tale of Laila and Majnu; *Shahnamah*, the great epic of ancient Persia; *Razmnamah*, the Persian translation of the *Mahabharata*; *Babarnamah*, the memoirs of his grandfather; and *Akbarnamah*, the history of his own rule.

"The works of all painters," according to Abul Fazl, "are weekly laid before His Majesty by the Darogah (supervisor) and the clerks. He then confers rewards according to the excellence of the workmanship, or he may increase the monthly salary. Much progress was made in the commodities required by painters, and the correct prices of such articles were carefully ascertained. The mixing of colors has especially been improved. The pictures thus received a hitherto unknown finish Excellent painters are now to be found in India, and masterpieces worthy of a Bihzad may be placed at the side of the wonderful works of European painters who have attained worldwide fame. The minuteness of detail, the general finish, and the boldness of execution now observed in pictures are incomparable; even inanimate objects look as if they have life. More than a hundred painters have become famous masters of the art, while the number of those who approach perfection, or those who are middling, is very large. This is especially true of the Hindus; their pictures surpass our conception. Few indeed in the whole world are equal to them."

As painting developed in the Mughal ateliers, it lost its purely Persian characteristics and became increasingly Indian. By the middle of Akbar's reign, the skies lost their gold and lapis-lazuli tones to break out into brilliant sunset colors. The stylized quality of Persian painting is replaced by movement and vigor, and the human figure becomes more and more Indian in feature and expression. Faces come alive showing that there was a close study of individual character traits. Miniatures became records of the emperor's activities: we see Akbar supervising the building of his dream city, Fatehpur Sikri; receiving the submission of a rebel; hunting tigers; receiving the manuscript of the *Ain-i-Akbari* from Abul Fazl; having a rebel thrown to his death; storming the forts and so on.

Basawan and Daswanth, Nanha and Bishan Das were some of the most famous painters of Akbar's court. Among the names mentioned in the *Ain-i-Akbari* are Kesu, Lal, Mukund, Mushkin, Tara, Sanwlah, Khemkaran, Madhu and Jagan. Bhagwati and Farrukh Beg also gained repute.

The Schools

Early Mughal art is purely masculine. The activities of women were never recorded. The portraits that are claimed to be of Mughal queens probably date from a later period, for all males, including the painters, were excluded from the Zanana, the women's quarters. Even Nur Jahan, Jahangir's wife, who indulged in such masculine activities as hunting and going to battle, did so on an elephant's back in a covered howdah. Jahangir lovingly describes one occasion when she shot two tigers with two shots and two others with four shots. On any similar occasion he would have summoned his painters to record the event, but in this case, he contented himself with writing about it and foregoing the visual record. Manucci, who spent some years in the country during the reign of Aurangzeb, had this to say. "I do not present any portraits of queens or princesses, for it is impossible to see them, since they are always concealed. If anyone has produced such portraits, they should not be accepted, being only likenesses of concubines and dancing girls, etc., drawn according to the artist's fancy."

From this it can be presumed that scenes of pleasure and dalliance with the ladies, which abound in later Mughal paintings, were also imaginary, the women portrayed being not the princesses themselves but the lesser attendants who moved freely in and out of the palaces and whose looks were no mystery to anyone.

Jahangir, Akbar's son had an advantage over his father in so far as he was left with a stable empire and could safely indulge in his favorite pastimes. He took delight in looking at works of art and paid tremendous prices for them. He was both patron and critic, and was capable of expressing an informed opinion on works of art. Sir Thomas Roe, the English ambassador at his court, describes an occasion when his own faith in the superiority of the artists of his own country was shaken. The ambassador had presented the emperor with a picture and was confident that no man in India could equal it. Jahangir asked him what he would pay the painter who could make such an exact copy that he would not be able to recognize his own. After some good-natured bantering, Roe was told to come again and see the pictures. He was shown six paintings and told to pick out his own. This he found difficult to do at first, and his initial failure delighted Jahangir. On another occasion, the emperor coveted a picture owned by the ambassador but would not accept it as a gift since it was the portrait of a dead friend and was of sentimental value to Roe. However, he asked the latter's permission to have it copied. Says Roe, "In that art of limning, his painters work miracles."

Indian Miniatures

Jahangir possessed an insatiable curiosity and had records made of all unusual objects and happenings. His painters, who accompanied him everywhere, made drawings of birds and animals which caught the emperor's eye. In his diary he writes, "Although King Babar described in his memoirs the appearance and shape of several animals, he never ordered the painters to make pictures of them. As these animals appeared to me very strange, I both described them and ordered that painters draw them for the *Jahangirnamah* so that the amazement arising from hearing about them might be increased." Mansur was the painter who excelled in animal subjects in Jahangir's time. The emperor's own knowledge, not only of painting but also of the technical excellence of his painters, was so great that he could tell who had done the eyes, the hands, the landscape, and so on. This was a time of specialization, and as Mansur was the specialist for birds and animals and Farrukh Beg for traditional Persian motifs, so others also had their specialties. In this reign the multiple signatures of the early reign disappeared and the miniature carried only one signature. Still later, the emperor's own expertise at guessing the artists put an end to the practice of affixing any signature to the work, and once again Indian painting became anonymous. The elimination of the signature, obviously, did not diminish the artist's worth in the emperor's eyes. When he heard of the death of Mir Imad, the renowned calligrapher at the Persian court, Jahangir wept. "If Shah Abbas had sent him to me," he is reported to have said, "I would have paid his weight in pearls for him."

In Jahangir's time, miniatures came to be made for preservation in folios rather than merely as book illustrations. Portraits became increasingly popular and Jahangir presented his portrait to all those he wished to honor. He also started the practice of having his courtiers wear miniatures of himself on a brooch that was attached to the front of the turban, a practice Shah Jahan followed. These are visible in some of the durbar scenes. Equestrian portraits, a purely Indian innovation since they are not found in Persian painting, were painted in great numbers.

The great love of the Mughals for creating gardens gave the painter a chance to study and paint various species of flowers. To these paintings he brings botanical expertise as well as an elevating sense of color and rhythm. These flower studies were made in large numbers during the reigns of Jahangir and Shah Jahan.

The reign of Shah Jahan was marked by a dazzling magnificence. The empire was now firmly established and the resources of the whole country were at the disposal of the "Great Mughal," who could indulge in his love of opulent display to his heart's content. The artists worked in the tradition of the earlier reign, but their work is distinguished by far greater use of gold and color. The miniatures, showing slightly overelaborate court scenes, are a reflection of the tastes of the builder of the Taj Mahal, "the poem in marble" that is considered one of the wonders of the world.

Together with the lavishness of the court is the ever-present mystic element. The stark realism of the earlier reign is replaced by scenes of holy men and portraits that reveal psychological insight, and the profile replaced the earlier three-quarters face. Even the durbar scenes show, with very few exceptions, rows of faces in profile.

The *siyah kalam*, or black and white drawings, sometimes lightly touched with gold and color, came into being. It was probably considered a more fitting medium for depicting certain moments and moods than the more opulent painting style. Works in this medium can be distinguished from mere sketches by the attention paid to detail and the finished quality of the works. The lines are thicker and more defined than those of the sketches and, quite often, only the face of the main figure is touched with color to make it stand out.

Shah Jahan's own love was architecture, and the beautiful buildings of his time are an index of his taste. Perhaps because his taste extended to the elaborate, the fabulous stone-encrusted Peacock Throne, on which the emperor sat, became a legend in his time, but the emperor did not seem to have taken any particular interest in painting. There is no record of the frank delight in art that his father found. It was inevitable, therefore, that from this time Mughal painting should show a definite decline. The delineation of detail, the fine brushwork and careful drawing are still present, but an element of stiffness and formalism forms a marked contrast to the fluid quality of the earlier miniatures.

Shah Jahan's son, Aurangzeb, was an ascetic whose philosophy of life did not tolerate frivolity or pleasures of any kind. He appointed a *muhtasib*, or censor of morals, to see that public life came up as close as possible to the precepts of Islam. He prohibited music and sternly discouraged styles of dress which he considered effeminate. Alcohol was forbidden and the cultivation of cannabis, known in India as *bhang*, was banned throughout the kingdom. The emperor himself led an extremely abstemious life, earning money for his personal expenditure by sewing caps and making copies of the Koran. He refused to allow any history of his reign to be written, perhaps as a precaution against self-idolization. While extremely simple in his private life, he nevertheless insisted on all the trappings of power, and the painters of his court were kept busy making visual records of his journeys, his durbars and other public occasions, and, of course, portraits.

While the emperor led an austere life in which even simple pleasures seemed to have no part, his courtiers indulged themselves in all sorts of extravagances. This is reflected in the painting of this period, which is full of music, drinking and love scenes, and although the scenes are rather contrived and the figures stiff, they continued to be painted during the succeeding reigns also. Techniques became looser, figures more rigid, lines less restrained and colors more garish as the Mughal empire headed toward decay.

As the empire declined the artists, too, traveled to other areas and sought patronage at other courts. Earlier, the courts that had alliances with the Mughals either had some Mughal artists working for them or had sent some of their own artists to be trained in the imperial ateliers. But now the better ones left the capital, carrying their own skills and ideas with them. This movement, combined with local idiom and tradition, gave rise to well-defined schools of painting all over the subcontinent. At the imperial capital itself, most of the works produced were either copies of the old or so much in the same tradition that there was very little individuality to them. The less talented artists set up stalls in the bazaars and made paintings that had no connection with the work ordered by the imperial patrons, often showing a remarkably primitive quality.

The outstanding seventeenth-century Mughal artists were Hunhar, Chitarman, Muhammad Nadir of Samarkand, Mir Mohammad Hashim, Goverdhan, Bhagwati, Anupchatar, Mansur, Manohar, Farrukh Beg and Abdul Hasan, Bichitr and Basawan.

MUGHAL USE OF PERSPECTIVE

The Mughal artist ingeniously combined the ancient Ajanta technique of perspective with that of contemporary Western artists. In the multiple perspectives used on ancient Buddhist frescoes, painters tried to suggest space by depicting figures simultaneously at eye level and from above, the direct view and the

The Schools

hierarchical perspective, placing figures in their order of importance and giving a kind of bird's eye view of the scene. By means of walls, rocks, cliffs and buildings, certain figures were brought into the foreground and others set in the distance. This form, combined with the European use of receding background, helped to give Mughal miniatures their perspective.

The drawing of cliffs, buildings and trees was replaced in the seventeenth century by groupings of minor characters arranged in semicircular form, leaving a distinct space for the main figure. In the Ajanta tradition, a thin line of shading encloses the outline of the figures. This becomes thicker and more prominent as a result of European influence, since color contrast was frequently used to lend relief, especially in the drawing of the head, which is pushed into prominence by the darker background.

The illusion of continuing space and action, created by cutting off a figure or building along the margins and in several other places, was a device used in Middle Eastern and sometimes in early Rajput miniatures. The Mughal miniatures make use of the same device. All the personages in the picture are connected by gesture, facial expression and proper positioning, and a harmonious balance is maintained in the composition.

The striving for harmony resulted in the depiction of individual parts of the body from different angles, with the legs and body in profile and the face in semi-profile and sometimes in reverse profile. The features of the face were also often portrayed from different angles.

MUGHAL DRESS

The male costume of the Mughals consisted of fitted pyjamas tied with a string at the waist, a long full-sleeved coat and a turban. The variations of this style of dress during succeeding reigns is an indication of the period of a picture.

1556–1605: The four- or six-pointed *jama*, or long coat, is found only in Akbar's time. The skirt was made up of four or six pointed pieces, allowing the edges to be tucked in at the waist during action. The emperor, however, disapproved of the style, and it went out of fashion, being replaced by a just-below-the-knee-length *jama* with a slightly scalloped effect along the hem and worn with a short sash.

1605–28: During Jahangir's period the *jama* is slightly longer and more pleated. The sash, too, is longer and wider, and is decorated with geometrical patterns.

The turban is large and loosely wound. Akbar and Jahangir both wore *jamas* of exceedingly fine muslim with practically no ornamentation.

1628–58: In Shah Jahan's period, we find that the *jama* became even longer and more thickly pleated. The sash is a little shorter and very elaborately decorated with floral designs. The material used is also thicker and more ornate than in the earlier reigns. The turban is elaborately tied with a very wide crossband.

1658–1707: The length and pleating of the *jama* remained the same during Aurangzeb's reign as in that of his predecessor, but the material became even thicker and more profusely patterned. The sash, slightly shorter and wider, continued to have floral patterns, while the crossband of the turban also became wider, giving the appearance almost of a cap.

1713–19: Aurangzeb's son, Farrukhsiyar, introduced a longer *jama* hanging to the ankle, fully pleated with a high waist. The sash and the turban conformed to the earlier modes.

1719–48: The *jama* became floor-length and the waistline crept up. The bodice and part of the skirt were ornamented. The fully pleated look continued. The turban was a variation of the two earlier styles, with the crossband having a different pattern.

The earlier miniatures mostly show women attired in Middle Eastern styles of dress, with here and there a typical Indian costume consisting of a skirt, bodice and scarf.

Middle Eastern dress consisted of a long gown covering the body from the neck to the ankles and wrists. A short-sleeved coat, often embroidered, cut straight at the top and gathered in at the waist, was worn over the garment. Sometimes a thick sheet was used to cover the head and shoulders.

Once in a while a woman is depicted wearing a fitting bodice and a skirt over trousers gathered at the waist and ankles. The head is covered, and in the case of queens, a crown is worn with a piece of cloth hanging from it and down the back. Stiff caps and turbans are often seen, and an oblong piece of cloth covers the head and hangs down to the shoulders.

The Mughal emperors married Rajput princesses, who are depicted in their own regional costume, consisting of an opaque bodice, a skirt with a sash and a scarf. By and large the maidservants are similarly dressed.

The Schools

By the middle of the seventeenth century, the Mughal women's costume had become quite similar to that of the men, consisting of a fitted bodice of gauzy material—often leaving the bosom bare—attached to a full skirt and worn over a pair of ornamented or striped tight pyjamas. A fine scarf covers the head and shoulders.

It is interesting to note that the *burqa*, an outer garment covering the whole body from head to toe, except for an inset of gauze around the eyes, was worn by many women in the early years of Muslim rule, and is still worn today.

POINTS TO REMEMBER

The earlier Mughal canvases teem with people engaged in various forms of activity. To distinguish an early Mughal miniature from its Persian counterpart, one has to look for less stylized and more realistic touches in human figures, animals and background. The depiction of underarm hair is an early Mughal characteristic, and the pointed *jama* appears only in early periods.

In the Jahangir period, the center of the picture is reserved for one or two important figures. The halo is a device used to distinguish the emperor from his subjects. Jahangir had his ears pierced in 1614, and pictures executed after that period always show him wearing earrings. There is an attempt to depict life as it is. People are shown engaged in building, carrying bricks, sawing planks of wood, plastering, sharpening axes, etc. Musicians, dancers, men slaughtering a mare or skinning a sheep, cooking and dishing out food, etc., are all depicted. Pictures of Jahangir's period are distinguished by a softness of color, a fineness of fabric and skin texture, and an extreme minuteness of detail.

The Shah Jahan period shows a tremendous use of gold, a lavishness of decoration and a slightly static quality. The fabrics are more opaque and decorated and the cusped arch makes an appearance. One finds enormous detail—differently patterned layers of fabric are clearly discernible—and there is more mobility than in later pictures.

The Mughal drawing is finer and the line surrounding the figures less visible than in any other school of painting. Figures, even at moments of greatest activity or statement of authority, are never stiff-necked. From the emperor to the lowest menial there is a slight bending forward and flexing of limbs that is not met elsewhere. Faces are oval with gently rounded planes, thus avoiding any harsh or abrupt lines. Hair is finely depicted with hundreds of brushstrokes, and fine featherlike shading gives depth to jaw and neck. Portraits try to give an insight into character rather than to represent the likeness of the subject. Especially noteworthy is the depiction of the hands, particularly in the Akbar and Jahangir periods. They are usually shown holding a flower, a sword, a hawk, the reins of a horse, or one hand is raised to make a point in a conversation. Even at rest they enhance the mood of the picture. Beards, which are almost completely absent in early Mughal painting, make an appearance during the reign of Shah Jahan and in later pictures.

Eighteenth-century miniatures are larger than the earlier ones. Women have a reddish brown tinge to their complexion, and grayish marble architecture is very prominent. Around 1750 there is a tendency to cover the face and throat with small blackish dots, thus giving the appearance of down. The cheeks, and sometimes the face, have a pinkish tint. In the latter part of the century, the subsidiary figures are drawn short and squat.

In the nineteenth century the static quality becomes very marked. There is a distinct Western influence in the colors and the modeling of planes, and the fine brushstrokes give way to filled-in surfaces.

PROVINCIAL MUGHAL

As the Mughal empire decayed, governors of various provinces declared themselves independent and assumed royal status. In the cultural tradition of the time they vied with one another in the sumptuousness of their living and their patronage of the arts. Painting flourished in their ateliers and, while retaining the dominant Mughal element, took on strong local color. Since most of the rulers who broke away from imperial rule were Muslims, there was no drastic break from the mainstream of art as it developed in Agra and Delhi.

MURSHIDABAD

As noted earlier the Pala kings of Bengal had been great patrons of art as well as of the crafts. The area was famous for its textiles—silks of various qualities—and the muslin produced at Dacca won world acclaim for its lightness and durability. The area around Dacca possessed an ideal humidity to allow a string of cotton to be pulled to a great length without breaking. Known by such lyrical names as *ab-e-rawan* ("flowing water"), a length of the woven material could easily be passed through an average-sized ring. It was so transparent that a cow is said to have eaten it along with the grass on which it was spread out to dry, and a Mughal emperor berated his daughter for appearing nude in his presence although she was draped in many layers of the material. The Mughals patronized the crafts, but the art of the area did not acquire any individuality until Bengal emerged from seclusion at the end of the seventeenth century, partly due to the weakening of the Mughal empire and the growth of European settlement and trade. In 1717, when Murshid Quli Khan was promoted to *subahdari* (governor) of Bengal, artists flocked to his flourishing capital of Murshidabad to work.

Early Murshidabad miniatures are very similar to those painted at the Mughal court during the reign of Aurangzeb. Later, however, the European influence becomes more noticeable, especially in the modeling of horses, the depiction of a face or a landscape. A number of dark, rounded bushes full of leaves or dotted with flowers is a characteristic of the region. In the second half of the eighteenth century, huge trees dwarfing the figures became a further characteristic of this school. The figures of this period are also slightly stumpy. After 1760, fine stippling on unnaturally gray or brownish white faces resulted in a slightly bloated expression.

After 1763, Muslim painting in Murshidabad fell into decline, surviving only through orders from the Hindu landed gentry or the British tradesmen. As in the Deccan, where later painting took on characteristics of the flourishing indigenous Dravidian art, so in Bengal it incorporated the characteristics of the local Kalighat folk art, along with those of Rajput art.

The portraits produced at the end of the eighteenth century show sharply chiseled features and the use of very thick lines to delineate the eyes. Other miniatures show small, squat figures, whose faces are modeled with graduated brown wash instead of the earlier stipple.

Direct European influence produced a new style of watercolor painting. Europeans, anxious to adorn their homes, commissioned Indian artists to paint for them. These pictures, meant to adorn walls, were of necessity larger than those meant for illustrating manuscripts, and the artist developed a new command of perspective and shading approximating European painting.

PATNA

Murshidabad painters migrated to Patna (now the capital of Bihar) around 1760. By the end of the century, this city became the headquarters of one of eleven areas into which the British East India Company divided Bengal. Here arose what is known as the "Company school" of painting, from the fact that its patrons belonged to the East India Company.

The young Victorian lady learnt to paint in watercolors as part of her education, and when she came out to India she made sketches of Indian scenes that interested her. Some of her men friends did the same, while others hired Indian artists to paint for them. These artists painted pictures of the service classes: washermen, tailors, maidservants, sweepers, basket makers and many others. These were made into lithographs and printed in books. Europeans had portraits of their families painted on paper, vellum, bone and ivory, while Indians demanded mythological scenes, records of marriages, etc.

The techniques of this painting, where the picture was painted with a brush without a pencil drawing, was known as *kajli siahi*, or black ink. The colors used are somber, deep sepia and ocher red, and contrast strongly with the white clothes of the figure. Subjects have pointed noses, heavy eyebrows, deep-seated, staring eyes and thin faces. There is a formalized look about the composition. Very little shading was used and modeling with stippling is frequent. Earlier pictures are drawn on paper produced locally or imported from Nepal, but later, European machine-made paper was used.

One of the painters of this school, Ishwari Prasad, became a professor at the School of Art in Calcutta, an organization responsible for modern painting in India.

Oudh

FAIZABAD AND LUCKNOW

In the second half of the eighteenth century, Oudh, a Mughal province, became very powerful under Nawab Shuja-ud-Daula (1753–75) and attracted many artists. Situated in the center of the fertile Gangetic plain, the area developed a culture of its own which reached its height under Wajid Ali Shah, the last ruler of Oudh, who was ousted from his throne by the British just before 1857.

The whole emphasis of life in Oudh was on etiquette and formality. Extreme norms of courtesy and elegance, combined with unlimited leisure, led to the evolution of an art that was replete with nuances. The famous Kathak dance that evolved in the court of Oudh is the most sensuous of all Indian dances, and implies as much as it states. Semiclassical music also reached a high degree of perfection here. The courtesans of Lucknow and Faizabad were noted for their grace and their refined tastes.

While retaining the basic Mughal style, the Oudh school developed a lavish style of its own, for there was a tremendous emphasis on decoration. Decanters are gem-encrusted, the spikes on the rails guarding flowerbeds have graceful twists and curls, and even the edges of the flowerbeds are decorated with swaying stems and flowers. Carpets are gorgeous, woven with scenes of hunting, and beds covered with magnificant bedspreads are placed under canopies.

The subject matter is usually the dalliance of lovers, and there is a possibility that some of the pictures were mere copies of older Mughal miniatures, but the embellishment and general treatment leave no doubt about their provenance.

The Oudh face is slightly different from the Mughal. The nose is bigger, with an outward thrust, and the features more clearly defined. The head is larger, with a thick growth of hair falling unfettered down the back. As if to offset their gorgeous surroundings, women wear few and simple ornaments. The *peshwaz*, a long dress with an opening at the collar, is sometimes worn by musicians and dancing girls.

THE DECCAN

The Vindhya Mountains, running east to west across the country have, until recent times, effectively divided India into two zones. Traditionally, invaders entered the country through the northwest, but their ranks and energies were so dissipated by the opposition they faced in the north that few managed to penetrate the peninsular area. The Deccan (from a Persian word meaning "south"), therefore, has maintained itself as a separate entity from the cultural melting-pot that was the north. Even the Muslim conquerors who set up kingdoms in the south were integrated into the culture of the people and enjoyed a comparatively more settled existence than their northern counterparts.

The tradition of wall paintings continued and flourished up until the great Hindu empire of Vijaynagar (fourteenth to sixteenth centuries), which was destroyed by the Bahmani kingdom in 1565. This, in turn, from a confederacy of five kingdoms—Berar, Bidar, Golconda, Bijapur and Ahmadnagar—became the three independent kingdoms of Golconda, Bijapur and Ahmadnagar, while Berar and Bidar were absorbed by them.

The two Hindu kingdoms of Vijaynagar and Orissa were obviously extremely rich in the tradition of art, but whereas Orissa paintings on palm leaf manuscripts have survived, no example of Vijaynagar miniature painting has ever come to light.

AHMADNAGAR, BIJAPUR AND GOLCONDA

Abul Muzaffar Yusuf Adil Shah, the founder of the Adil Shahi dynasty (1490–1686) of Bijapur, was the son of one of the Ottoman emperors of Asia Minor. He invited artists to his court from Persia and the Middle East. His son, Ismail Adil Shah, like Jahangir in the north, was an adept painter, and another descendant, Ibrahim Adil Shah (1580–1627), was a master of calligraphy and painting. European influence reached the area through Goa and the Coromandel Coast.

As we have already seen, the Malwa manuscript of *Nimatnamah*, a cookery book, represents a cross between Gujarati and Middle Eastern traditions. The paintings have a sweeping quality that makes figures more curvaceous and gives animation to flowers, birds and human figures not found in Jain manuscripts.

The *Nujum-ul-Ulum* ("Book of Sciences"), which deals with astronomy, painted in Bijapur in about 1570, shows the same foreign elements in combination with the existing traditions of Vijaynagar fresco painting.

Female figures are long-waisted and lean, clad in sarees with long folds. The heads are usually too small for the length of the figures. The head is either covered or bare, and the hair is done in a chignon, often decorated with flowers. Foreheads are very low, and flat crowns slope into luxuriant masses of hair. The hands are like stumps when clenched, and when open, the fingers protrude like little sticks. The feet are also disproportionately small, and seem hardly able to bear the weight of the body.

The strong drawing and the vibrant colors of the figures, placed against pastel backgrounds, imbue them with fierce power and strength. The formal stance is indicative of tremendous vitality and power, and the faces, always in profile, strengthen the sense of purpose. The firm mouth, the slightly double chin, not with fat but with determination, and the slightly hooked nose all add up to a

The Schools

sternness of character and a dedication that is almost sublime. The curly clouds, the clusters of grass and plants of different sizes are essentially Persian, but later become indigenous to Deccan painting.

The *Tarif-i-Hussain Shahi* was written and illustrated at Ahmadnagar roughly around the same time as the *Nujum-ul-Ulum*. The most outstanding of its illustrations shows the Dohada ceremony, in which a tree bursts into flower when embraced by a beautiful and chaste woman, or touched with her foot.

The figures are set in what appears to be an alcove, judging by the blue background and the golden top. The bodies are elongated, with narrow foreheads and sloping heads similar to those in the *Nujum-ul-Ulum*. However, the features and stances are quite different—the women have pliable natures and mellower temperaments. Hands, feet and head are more in proportion, and the hair hangs in a long plait down the back. The middle figure, the queen, differs from the others in that she is less sinuous and more squat, and shows power and authority in her expression. Men's necks are drawn uncommonly long and columnlike, and the shape of the turban emphasizes the pointed shape of the head. Paintings of Ibrahim Adil Shah II (1580–1626) of Bijapur and his retinue show heads and faces somewhat too small and narrow for the bodies.

The tree bursting into flower, cypresses and the blue background are all Persian characteristics, while the banana tree, the palm, the clothes and ornaments and, above all, the subject itself, are purely Indian.

By the end of the sixteenth century, women's clothes changed from the saree to the skirt, bodice and *dupatta*, a piece of cloth covering the head, shoulders and bosom, and the heavy chignon gave way to the long plait. The scarf was of fine embroidered or printed material projecting in stiff winglike angles.

It is not possible to clearly define the work done in the different centers of the Deccan as the volume of works produced there is not large and the characteristics not as marked as in the Pahari or Rajasthani schools. Except in the case of portraits of various nobles, which can be presumed to have been painted in their capitals, the rest can be placed under the general heading of the Deccan school.

The Golconda male was dressed in long, flowing robes wider at the bottom than the Mughal robe. The half-sleeved overcoat with a fur collar is a distinguishing feature of this area.

A fashion of Golconda and Bijapur, but not of Ahmadnagar, was the use of long, wide straps at the sides of the coat. The looped girdles of the attendants are also a feature of the Golconda style, as is the lavish display of utensils. In Ahmadnagar the attendants wore a rectangular flap made of gold filigree and suspended from one side of the girdle.

Burhan, the youngest son of the hero of the *Tarif-i-Hussain Shahi*, rebelled against his brother Murtaza I and sought refuge at the Mughal court of Akbar, where he stayed for eight years, returning in 1591 to rule Ahmadnagar. It was through him that Mughal influence reached Deccan painting. In 1600 he was defeated, but the kingdom survived under the brilliant leadership of Malik Ambar (1549–1626), who kept the Mughals at bay. The Mughal element in painting and other arts, however, continued to develop, and intermarriage and general cultural exchanges made the Mughal style current in the Deccan. Both Bijapur and Golconda artists were influenced by Mughal techniques, but their work cannot be compared with that of the north in naturalism, as it is always endowed with a mystic and spiritual quality.

HYDERABAD

By 1688, Golconda, Bijapur and Ahmadnagar were all absorbed by the Mughal empire. In 1724, Asaf Jah I overthrew Mughal suzerainty to found the independent Asaf Jahi dynasty, which favored the arts.

Although the Hindu influence in *fakirs*, *sadhus* and women had become noticeable in the intervening years between the fall of the empire and the rise of Hyderabad, in Hyderabad paintings of the mid-eighteenth century, we find that the subject matter is closely related to Mughal painting of the late seventeenth century. Even so, the dress, the arrangement of figures, the typical Deccan background and the often depicted poppy flowerbeds leave no doubt about where the picture was painted. By the end of the eighteenth century, pictures became more ornate, with a distinct penchant for portraiture and harem scenes. Hunting scenes, a great favorite with the Mughals, are seldom met with in the Deccan.

Late eighteenth-century portraiture shows a profile set against a flat background of light green or blue, with a small band of tangled clouds at the top and a flat wash of darker color or a series of formal flowerbeds at the bottom. Jewelry is ornate, and consists mostly of pearls. A long robe is worn over a long *choli*, or bodice, and striped, plain or floral patterned pyjamas. *Dupattas* are transparent and may cover

The Schools

the head and shoulders, or may be draped over the shoulders and across the chest. The latter are known as *khara dupatta*, a typical Deccan style. The swaying movement of the *dupatta* is also typically Deccan.

Men wear long, plain or flowered muslin *jama* that touch the ankles, narrow cummerbunds and low, small turbans. Trousers are usually pale red in color. Men of rank wore jewelry.

Hashia, or the borders of miniatures, up to 1750 have golden floral designs on cinnabar red grounds; after 1750, they are mostly plain and vermilion in color.

The architecture is typical of late Mughal and Deccan style. Flowerpots of white and blue Chinese design are popular. Long-stemmed glass bottles are displayed in niches as in Mughal and Rajasthani miniatures.

The paintings executed at the command of the Hindu officials of the rulers are entirely Hindu in costume and subject matter. They were mostly done by Hindu painters from Tanjore or Shorapur and show the subject worshiping a deity, engaged in conversation with saints (including Guru Nanak, founder of the Sikh religion in the north), or depict scenes from the Hindu epics. Some were painted for Gujarati merchants. These closely resemble works of the Rajasthani and Pahari schools.

Some characteristics of the Hyderabad school are as follows. Scenes are usually depicted on a terrace outside the building, with a pavilion in the background, or in a garden with willow, mango, *champa* (*Michelia champaka*), coconut or palm trees. Quite often there is a fringe of lighter colored leaves around the trees. Formal flowerbeds with poppies and other flowers are arranged on either side of a rectangular pool in which fishes and ducks may be seen. Flower petals are depicted by slightly raised dots.

The sky is usually a dull blue or a yellow or blue-green, at the upper edge of which clouds are depicted by golden or indigo streaks. Often a small band of clouds runs along the top of the picture.

The wide terraces are covered with cushions and floral patterned carpets in yellow, red, green or mauve. Cushions are often embroidered or woven in gold brocade, or made of the patterned *himru* silk of Hyderabad.

The parapets of the terraces are either of marble or golden or red wooden balustrades. Doors are light brown with veins of darker brown or black running through them. Male and female figures are tall and well built. Women's foreheads are sloping and their hair is brushed well back and off the face.

SOUTH INDIAN PAINTING

The term "South Indian" painting indicates the Hindu or Hindu influenced school of art as opposed to the basically Muslim schools of the Deccan.

The rulers of the south were great patrons of the arts, as is evidenced by the elaborately carved caves and the huge temples that are found all over the area. As in the north no paintings as such dating before the twelfth century have been found there, but the fragments of painting left in caves and temples give an indication of the excellence achieved. As painting moved diagonally across the peninsular area, from northwest to southeast, Ajanta to Tanjavur, facial features underwent a marked change and took on the Dravidian characteristics of the indigenous population. These are a decidedly square lower lip, a heavy jaw, a pointed, hooked nose, long eyes and steeply arched eyebrows.

Palm leaf Jain manuscripts found at Moodbidri, a Jain religious center, therefore differ markedly from those made in Gujarat. The leaves are unusually large, and there is less stylization. The line is much more rounded and the figures lack the fierce vitality of their Gujarat counterpart. The panels separating the text from the pictures are decorated with bold lines in geometric, floral or scroll patterns, sometimes giving an impression of a textile border or pottery decoration. There is a folk look to the works.

Between the fourteenth and seventeenth centuries, the Vijaynagar empire, which renounced Muslim rule, was the dominant power in the Deccan. Many temples were built and decorated with sculpture and painting. During this period, figures are shown to be well built, with pronounced hips in both males and females. There is a marvelous degree of ornamentation in the clothes, which are depicted in a swirl of lines, circles, dots and flowers. The saree is very prominent, and is draped either to cover or reveal the breasts. Hair is luxuriant and worn in a huge chignon or a long plait. The head, except when covered with a crown, is bare.

The Nayaka kings of Tanjavur and Madurai, who ruled southeast India from the sixteenth to eighteenth centuries, also fostered art in their courts. The line is finer and the figures longer and more elegant. The wide-open eye, though, imparts a sense of fierceness to the figures. The three lines around the neck and the depiction of the chin by a circle are prominent. Here also, there is a wealth of ornamentation.

In a miniature showing scenes from the *Ramayana*, the whole is divided into horizontal panels, which in turn are divided into areas, each displaying a different scene. The whole work is prevented from becoming overcrowded by keeping ornamentation down to a minimum. The distinctive crown, the men's style of wearing their hair, with the front of the head shaved and the hair wound in a stiff knot at the back, the women's sarees and, of course, the writing make it impossible for this south Indian picture to be confused with any product from the north.

Venkoji, the stepbrother of Sivaji, conquered Tanjavur and brought the Marhatta influence there. The paintings of this area, from the eighteenth century onward, are characterized by pure color, with slight modeling effected by shading the inside of the contour. The favorite colors are red, blue, black, white and yellow. Jewels, drapery and architectural details are slightly raised by means of a special paste made of fine sawdust and glue, carefully modeled and covered with gold leaf after fixing in semiprecious stones or pieces of multicolored glass. Figures are heavy and stylized and lack movement, with the principal figure larger than the rest. Themes are religious and make the pictures proper objects of worship.

DIFFERENCES BETWEEN DECCAN AND MUGHAL PAINTINGS

The similarity of style between seventeenth-century and later court paintings of north and south India resulted in the works being classified under the term "Mughal." The two schools, however, show marked differences and are clearly the products of entirely different regions and cultural orientation.

Portraits occupy a very important place in Deccan painting. They are shown in profile, or three-quarters of the face is usually set against a background of either light color wash or the natural tone of the paper. Sometimes a deep blue sky with a few curling clouds and small flowering shrubs embellish the tops and bottoms of the pictures. Their similarity to Mughal portraits is marked, but a second glance shows that the portraits produced in the Deccan are more positive and clearly defined, and lack the psychological insights of the former.

One very vital difference between Mughal and Deccan painting is in the amount of decoration used. Deccan miniatures are lavishly ornamented, and all available space in the background is filled in with flowering shrubs, trees, carpets or buildings. Clothes are decorated with gold, as are seat bolsters, utensils and even pillars. Mughal miniatures have much simpler settings.

Clothes are differently fashioned; especially notable is the formalized twist to the ends of sashes and skirt hems in the Deccan. Men's clothes in the Deccan are usually more ornamented than Mughal clothes and the *jama* are of opaque, patterned material. Even where the material is fine, it is quite often patterned, with decorated seams and edges. A shawl may cover the shoulders, or a long coat worn, its three-quarter length sleeves trimmed with fur. A long piece of fur is also worn around the neck. The straight gold belt of the Deccan is never found in Mughal fashions.

Female facial characteristics are also different. The Mughal face, whether round or oval, is always an aristocratic one, without harshness, the planes gentle and rounded into a smoothly pleasant whole. Character is not lacking, but it is character mellowed by long breeding and a gentle mode of life. The forehead is high, the nose aquiline, eyebrows arched, mouth small and firm and chin rounded. The hair falls unhampered down the back. More or less the same description can be applied to the Deccan women, although there is a definite vigor here. The forehead rises sharply from the ridge of the nose, the hair is not pulled back leaving the forehead free but is softly waved on each side to reduce the height and width of the forehead.

In another Deccan facial type, the hair is pulled back tightly to reveal a high-domed forehead. In certain pictures Deccan characteristics are toned down to make them appear Mughal, but the Deccan figure is always a definite statement of vigor, vitality and earthiness absent in the Mughal.

Deccan birds and animals are much more fiercely alive than Mughal ones. The struggle for survival seems to have caught the imagination of the southern artist more than his northern counterpart, who was much more impressed with the more amenable qualities of birds and beasts. The vibrant southern colors add to the quality of vitality.

Another difference of detail is found in Deccan vases. Set in wall niches, they are long and narrow with short necks; Mughal and Rajasthan ones are shorter and broader with longer necks.

Whereas from an early date Mughal artists assimilated the Persian element

The Schools

and made it entirely their own, in Deccan works the two elements remained entirely separate. In many cases, the figures are almost totally Middle Eastern, while the surroundings, i.e., the chairs, the pattern on the carpet, the flowering shrubs, and above all, the colors—vermilion, crimson, orange, green, gold, azure, violet and pink—are all unmistakably Deccan. For some reason, Deccan artists seemed to envisage important persons having Mongol features. Even portraits of Mughal emperors done by Deccan artists feature such strong Mongol touches that they are almost unrecognizable. The faces are delicately pale and the figures stiff.

THE RAJPUT SCHOOLS

An area of approximately 350,000 square miles, partly desert, was termed Rajputana by the British, otherwise known colloquially as Rajwarra and by the sophisticated as Raethana, or "place of kings." (The original Rajputana has been broken up, and part of it is now called Rajasthan.) It was divided into princely states of varying sizes and strengths, which belonged to dynasties claiming descent from the sun and moon and boasting such forebears as Rama of *Ramayana* fame.

These autocratic monarchs belonged to the *kshatriya*, or warrior, caste and lived and died by a certain code. The honor of a Rajput was inviolate and any threat to it had to be staved off with his life. A promise once given could never be taken back but had to be honored at any cost.

In battles the Rajput army fought to the last and the men would gladly die rather than return home defeated. The women were as fiercely proud as the men and refused to welcome back a defeated husband. Stories are told of a warrior who returned home wounded, only to be told by his wife that she did not recognize him since her husband would never have been cowardly enough to return home after a defeat. Shamed, the warrior fell on his sword and took his own life.

While the battle raged, the women would watch its progress from the ramparts of the fort. When they felt that the day was lost, they would retire to a special room for self-immolation. This room had a pit in the center for the fire and a single door which was locked when the fire was lit. Suspended from the high ceiling were a number of swings. The women, dressed in their best, seated

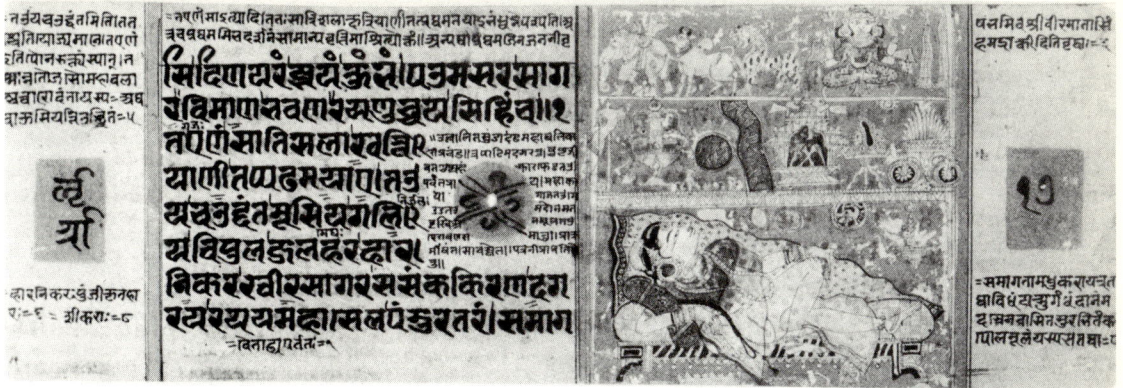

41. *Jain*. Early 15th century. The sixteen dreams of Trisala. Trisala lies at the bottom of the picture while all the beautiful and fantastic things she dreams about are ranged above her. The drawing is extremely fine, without the fierceness that was to become a feature of later Jain painting.

42. *Mughal*. Late 16th century. An amorous couple. The woman's draperies are so transparent as to be almost invisible. There is strong underarm shading. The border decoration is Persian in character.

43. *Mughal.* Late 16th century. A page from the *Sikandarnamah*, the history of Alexander the Great. Alexander sits on a throne receiving gifts and homage. The general composition of the picture, the minute details in the drawing, and the foreground are all Persian, but the Indian influence is visible in some of the figures and the style of dress.

44. *Malwa.* Late 17th century. Mughal influence is apparent in the greater sophistication of the drawing, the ornamentation and the presence of underarm shading. The eye has shrunk to almost natural proportions, although it is still prominent. The change becomes obvious if this picture is compared with plate 5.

45. *Mughal*. Late 16th century. Portrait of Tan Sen, the famous musician. The drawing is extremely fine, and the subject emerges with his own distinctive personality. The slight bend of the body marks him out to be an artist as well as a courtier.

46. *Mughal* Early 17th century. Man with a melon. The main picture is of this date. The involvement of the man with cutting the melon is total, and the background is very finely drawn. The border, however, is of a later date. The drawing is bold and less natural, and the birds and animals are quite lifeless.

47. *Mughal.* Middle 17th century. Prince paying homage to an ascetic. This is a good study in expressions—the remoteness of the holy man, the awe on the prince's face and the ecstasy on that of the musician who is transported by his own music. Such pictures abound in the Mughal school and this one has all the usual characteristics: delicate lines, transparent draperies and a landscape providing depth.

48. *Mughal*. Early 18th century. Woman feeding a pet fox. The floral fabric of the pyjamas and the striped bodice are clearly visible through the *jama* and the draperies. The brushstrokes are no longer as fine as in earlier pictures, but there is a sense of restraint in the veiling of the heavily decorated garment to avoid over-ornamentation, a feature of late Mughal painting.

49. *Mughal*. Late 18th century. Girls dancing. This theme is also met with in other schools. In earlier paintings, the girls' faces would have registered enjoyment, but here they are serious and decorous, as if not really concerned with what they are doing. The brushwork and modeling are also evidence of the late date of the picture.

50. *Mughal.* Middle 17th century. A lion carted off after the hunt. The lion occupies the major part of the picture, its dead weight bearing down heavily on the men, who carry the animal on poles. Mughal natural-ness has here been deeply influenced by the Hindu hierarchic perspective, where the main figure dwarfs everything around it.

51. *Ahmadnagar*. Circa 1600. Malik Ambar. The soldierly qualities of the subject are conveyed by his bull-like neck and his strong physique. The small head is a pre-Mughal Deccan characteristic. Note the baglike object through which the sash is looped.

52. *Bijapur*. Late 16th or early 17th century. Man on horseback. Despite the ornamentation in the picture and the decoration on the border, the composition has a strong primitive look. The thousands of brushstrokes used for the beard, the dappled horse and the falcon do not prevent the impression of filled-in surfaces.

53. *Deccan.* Late 18th century. Lady and her maidens listening to music. The women sit on a terrace with a spectacular view of the countryside. The whole picture is beautifully decorated, the bolster and cushion being covered in the brocade of the area. The stiff *dupatta* veil worn by the lady is characteristic of the Hyderabad region.

54. *Deccan*. Late 18th or early 19th century. Meeting of lovers. A secluded corner cut off by rocks shelters the lovers, while the attendants wait patiently for the tryst to be over. Such pictures are found in all schools.

55. *South Indian*. Middle 19th century. Portrait of a south Indian nobleman. The European influence is very evident, both in the pose and the execution of the picture. The caste mark on the forehead, the headdress and jewelry reveal its provenance.

56. *Mewar*. Early 17th century. Some great poets of the Bhakti cult. The faces are obviously imaginary, but they are convincingly drawn. The characteristics of Mewar—boldness in the drawing, long eyes and primary colors—are all there, but the picture is unusual for the white background and pastel shades instead of the usual vibrant colors.

57. *Kishangarh*. Early 18th century. Prince hunting buffalo. Although the buffalo is mortally wounded and there is much wielding of swords, the picture lacks life. Even the horse on the left, which has one leg around the quarry's neck, seems to be standing still. Only the elongated figure on horseback gives an indication of the way the school would develop in a few years.

58. *Marwar.* Early 18th century. King with his consort. The decoration, mainly on the clothes and the carpet, is restrained. Note the tree trunks showing through the trellis work. As is usual in Rajasthani painting, the figures are projected against a plain background.

59. *Kishangarh*. Middle 18th century. Krishna, dressed as a woman, approaches Radha, seated on a throne and dressed as a man. The attendants, musicians and the women in the boats letting off fireworks fill the canvas, but are unable to disturb the total involvement of the two. Krishna is distingnishable by the blue tint of his face and Radha by the presence of breasts. Note also the resemblance of all the figures to the two.

60. *Jaipur*. Middle 18th century. Portrait of Raja Singh (1729–68). There is no character insight to the subject, but the look of authority and, of course, the halo, mark him as a ruler. The background is plain, but the symmetrical clouds at the top of the picture pick up the formal design on the *jama*, giving the picture a decorative appearance.

61. *Jodhpur*. Middle 18th century. The month of the rains—one of a *Baramasa* series. The stiff skirts, the high sloping foreheads, the rounded, almost swollen cheeks and arching eyebrows are characteristics of this school. Note the streaks of lightning visible through the falling rain at the top of the picture.

62. *Rajasthan*. Late 18th century. King with his consort petting a deer. The powerful lines of the king's body contrast with the petite delicacy of his queen, who has a doll-like appearance. Although most painters depicted male and female figures in proportion to each other, some used this device to emphasize the qualities of masculinity and femininity and the power and protecting capacity of the male.

63. *Rajasthan folk*. Late 18th century. Durga killing a demon. There is a sense of elemental energy in this picture. Even the trees seem to be showering wrath on the villain. The use of beetles' wings in the goddess's ornaments may lead to the conclusion of a Basohli provenance, but a closer study shows that it was done in Rajasthan.

64. *Kishangarh.* Early 19th century. Princess enjoying fireworks with her maidens. This is a good example of the development of most schools: the individual characteristics that distinguished the school are gone and the work could be from anywhere in Rajasthan. The elaborate tapestry and over-ornamentation of the picture point to a late date.

65. *Rajasthan folk*. Middle 18th century. Rama, Lakshmana and Sita reach a hermitage during their wanderings in the forest. The lines of the flowing river and the trees full of flowers relieve the static quality in the picture.

66. *Jaipur*. Early 19th century. Radha and Krishna throwing dice. The heavy brushwork, the stiff draperies, the slightly contrived pose and the excessive use of ornamentation all reveal the late date of this picture.

67. *Rajasthan*. Middle 19th century. Malstri Ragini, wife of Shree
Raga. The over-ornamentation of the picture, the lack of proper
proportions and the clumsy drawing are all indications of the late
date of this miniature.

68. *Kota*. Middle 19th century. There is a strong folk element in this picture. The animals seem to be made of clay, and the hectic activity in which they are engaged seems contrived. The falling figure in the center has the look of a puppet whose strings have been loosened.

69. *Jodhpur*. Early 19th century. The rearing horse, the fan-like spread of clothes, the long heavy-lidded eyes are all characteristics of this school. The late date is evident from the stylized modeling of the horse, the poor proportions of the figures and the large-scale drawing.

70. *Guler*. Middle 18th century. This is a portrait of Raja Bishen Singh (1744–73), the elder brother of Raja Govardhan Chand of Guler.

71. *Basohli*. Middle 18th century. Kamodi Ragini. The composition is stylized, although not nearly so much as in earlier pictures, and there is a distinct softening of line and expression. Although the figures cannot be said to be natural, they are not as angular or as elongated as before.

72. *Pahari*. Late 18th century. Battle between gods and demons. The Hindu concept of giving important figures their due place is very prominent here. Three figures dwarf all others, including an elephant, although they are all on the same plane.

73. *Pahari*. First half of 19th century. King with his attendant. The clothes, the stance of the figures, the hookah, the facial features and style of turban are all unmistakeably Pahari, but it is not possible to pinpoint the school for lack of special characteristics.

74. *Bilaspur.* Early 19th century. Krishna lifting the mountain. This type of picture could be from anywhere except for certain pointers: the purposeful stance of the figures, the headdress of the cowherds and the cattle, which lead us to conclude that it is from Bilaspur, despite the absence of the gnarled tree.

75. *Kangra school*. Second quarter of the 19th century. Vipralabdha Nayika—the jilted heroine. She stands dejected by a pond into which she throws her ornaments. The figure is delicately proportioned, but the face is disproportionately large, as are the hands. The ground is made up of innumerable fine lines and some stippling.

76. *Kangra*. Middle 19th century. Radha and Krishna. The faces are well proportioned and Radha has the usual dulcet charm of this school. However, the picture lacks refinement; its filled-in surfaces, heavy brushwork, lack of detail on the border and clumsy flattening at the sides to make it fit the border all point to its late date.

77. *Kangra*. End of 19th or early 20th century. Village scene. This seems to be an earlier picture that has been added to later. The faces of the men are alive and are well drawn, made up of fine strokes. The two women on the left are also reasonably proportioned though not so well modeled. But the woman on the right, the buildings and the foreground are later additions. Note the apple, grapes and mangoes in the niches on the wall—a rather unusual feature.

78. *Company school*. Middle 19th century. The artist has managed to catch the sense of movement of the surprised bird. The wing feathers are minutely depicted, like ornamental looped curtains.

79. *Pahari*. Late 19th century. The earlier fine proportions and delicate brushwork of Pahari painting have given way to this squat, disproportionate figure with filled-in surfaces and a solid modeling of face and clothes.

themselves on the swings and as they moved higher would let go of the rope and fall into the fire. When a Rajput died a natural death, his wife mounted the funeral pyre willingly and with grace.

Fighting was almost considered a religious duty for the Rajputs, and they spent their lives in this pursuit, either fighting one another or foreign invaders. Throughout the Mughal rule the Rajputs fought their kin on different sides during the imperial battles of succession. Since the Muslims had no law of primogeniture, it was inevitable that all the sons of a ruler would fight for the throne. The Rajput participation in these battles of succession is easily explained when one studies the genealogy of the Mughal princes. The mother of one of Jahangir's sons, for example, was a princess of Marwar, while that of another son was from Amber. When the two princes fought each other, their kinsmen automatically sided with them.

The nomenclature of the various Rajput states as they exist today is a legacy of the British, who named the states after the capital cities rather than after the principality itself. Thus Mewar and Marwar are known as Udaipur and Jodhpur, while Kota and Bundi are the names used for the region of Haravati, and Jaipur the name given to the area of Dhoondar.

These areas were governed by the fabled maharajas, rulers of a great many of the principalities of India with whom the British made treaties. They gained fame in the Western world for their magnificent and sometimes decadent living styles, but their romantic and chivalrous background is little known. Although divested of all power by the Indian government, and with it their titles, they are still Maharaja (Great Ruler) and Maharani (Great Queen) to their retainers and their people, who still remain loyal to them.

The color sense of the Indian is justly famed. Every area has its traditional colors which complement the natural background and make the people stand out from their surroundings. Thus, in Kerala, the lush green of the countryside is emphasized by the stark whiteness of the people's clothes. Rajasthan is the great color belt of India, and every costume is a sumptuous delight. Red, green, ocher, saffron, purple and magenta all form a living, moving palette standing out sharply from and yet blending in with the background. The same enthusiasm for color is to be found in the painting of the region. Rajput painters made as much use as possible of primary colors, which they managed to blend onto a single canvas.

The Schools

Tie and dye is the main Rajput method of decorating fabrics for clothes. This process results in a vast variety of patterns on a piece of material. The design can be achieved in a single color or in many hues. Geometrical patterns, flora and fauna decorate sarees and other garments. There are different designs for all occasions—a wedding, the birth of a boy, the birth of a girl, Holi, Divali, the rainy season, spring and every festival. The patterns are evident in the painting of the area and of the schools influenced by it.

Between the Jain and the Mughal periods, the style of painting in these areas formed a halfway house bridging the two schools. The protruding eye of the Jain disappeared, but the eye was drawn so long that it touched the ear and was wide open. Faces were in profile and heads flat, while clothes were decorated with stripes, dots, stars and flowers. Plain, disc-shaped earrings were worn by both men and women. Architecture was represented by a small, single-storied building, canopied, with slender pillars. There was a folk look to the whole composition and the drawing lacked finish and sophistication, but the former stylization was replaced by a new naturalism.

The particular miniature that is known as Rajput or Rajasthani, however, came into being only after the seventeenth century, when the flourishing Mughal school fused with the existing Jain school to produce a style of its own. After the initial struggle, the earlier Mughal emperors sought alliances with Rajput princes and appointed them to high positions at court. Rajput princesses entered Mughal harems, bringing their own culture with them. This synthesis produced, as has been noted earlier, some of the most aesthetically appealing and enduring art forms ever seen.

The flourishing ateliers of the Mughals had already set the style, and local artists in various states, where patronage and distinct art forms already existed, soon produced a new style of art. The court art of the Mughals was assimilated into the predominantly folk art of the area, resulting in paintings which resembled the products of Delhi and Agra.

The innately hierarchical concept of art and the mystic bent of the Hindu mind predominated, edging out the realistic approach of the pragmatic Muslim. The Rajasthani artist followed traditions laid down in the early treatises and imbued each piece he produced with a deeper significance. Each figure, tree or animal became a symbol to convey an emotion rather than to depict a mere incident.

Indian Miniatures

A notable feature of Hindu painting is that the figures, even when they occupy a small portion of the surface, always dominate the scene. The surrounding scenery, and any birds or animals that may be depicted, relate to the figures and serve to underscore the situation rather than to provide a naturalistic background.

This total absorption in the mystical rather than the visual significance of the picture made the Rajput artist use his space in a very unorthodox manner, without any attempt at naturalism. Quite often the figures in the distance are not necessarily the smallest, and perspective is often used as a device for emphasizing atmosphere rather than obtaining verisimilitude.

Even in actual portraits of rulers and nobles, costume, background and pose all give visual evidence of the capability and character of the subject. A sword indicates martial prowess, while a flower is a clue to more aesthetic and pleasant pursuits. The powerful shape of a horse may be an index of the dignity and might of its owner. Certain pictures show horses with heads draped with cloth that is sewn and embroidered to resemble the head of an elephant. This enhanced the grandeur of the owner and gave him the prestige of seeming to ride a majestic elephant that had the mobility of a horse. In many portraits it is difficult to tell whether one is looking at the likeness of a real person or the depiction of a *raga*. Quite often the raja is depicted as Krishna, and the scene is imbued with a deeply religious significance.

Shading is not nearly as pronounced in Rajput as in Mughal miniatures. A thick line was used for emphasis or to model faces, and shadowing along the contours usually sufficed to depict depth. On a human face, shading served more to convey expression than to give volume.

Unlike Mughal miniatures, Rajput miniatures are decorously enclosed within their frames. There is seldom any attempt to depict continuing action by cutting off figures from the borders or by drawing cliffs. Colors are much more vivid, primary ones being favored. Figures are generally projected against a plain, contrasting background.

In earlier miniatures, vividly colored areas divided the background into irregular quadrangles. Later these were replaced by smaller accents of intense color. Black, orange and red, the colors of life and love, predominate. The flesh tones of ordinary figures are replaced, in the case of Krishna, by a blue-gray. This color, a little more gray than blue, is also used to depict Vishnu and some of the ascetics.

The Schools

There was considerable movement of both art and artists between the many Rajput states, and illustrated manuscripts and paintings formed part of the dowries of princesses. Certain kingdoms which patronized the arts produced works with clearly defined characteristics, but the bulk of the paintings can only be generally termed Rajput, since the artists of some areas did not have enough individuality to put their own impress on their works.

The best examples of each school stand out clearly and have strong individual characteristics. Certain colors and motifs characterize each of them, but by and large, the difference is most noticeable in the facial features. A study of the shapes of the nose, eyes and eyebrows and height of the forehead makes it easy to differentiate between the paintings of various areas.

In eighteenth- and early nineteenth-century paintings, the inscription on top gives the name of the king or nobleman depicted and often mentions the name of the artist and the date of the work. The outstanding Rajput schools are Mewar, Jaipur, Jodhpur, Bikaner, Bundi, Kotah and Kishangarh.

MEWAR

The history of Mewar is one of the most stirring in the annals of India. Its rulers bore the title "Rana" and were the elder branch of the Suryavansi, or "the children of the sun," family. They traced their descent from Rama, hero of the *Ramayana*, and held precedence over the other Rajput tribes. Mewar is one of the two Rajput kingdoms whose boundaries have remained the same through eight centuries of foreign domination. The rulers were men of outstanding courage and determination, who managed for centuries to hold off the gradual domination of the kings of Agra and Delhi.

The impregnable fort of Chittorgarh withstood repeated attacks from invaders, becoming a beacon of honor for all Rajputs, embodying their chivalry, gallantry and intrepidity. In the thirteenth century, Chittor, according to Colonel Tod, "the repository of all that was precious and yet untouched of the arts of India," was sacked by Alauddin Khilji, the ruler of Delhi. The latter was smitten by tales of the beauty of Padmini, wife of the regent of Chittor during the minority of the ruler. Alauddin laid siege to the fort and demanded possession of the lady. Later he toned down his request and asked for a single glimpse of her. He was allowed to enter the fort and look at Padmini's reflection in a mirror. On leaving the fort, he captured the regent and demanded Padmini as ransom for his release. After a battle in which the regent and his bravest warriors were killed, the lady burned herself and the fort fell into the hands of the Khiljis.

It was recaptured in the next century and the area under its jurisdiction was as large as before. Mewar reached the summit of its glory under the sixteenth-century ruler Rana Sanga, who headed the Rajput confederacy to oppose Babar, the first Mughal emperor. He was defeated and retreated, but was not pursued by Babar, who never forgave himself for this lapse. Finally, the fort fell before the might of his grandson, Akbar, who forced Rana Udai Singh to flee to the valley of the Aravalli Hills, where some years previously he had built the Udai Sagar, the lake named after him.

Rana Pratap, his successor, waged guerrilla warfare against the Mughal empire, harassing the rulers for twenty-five years and spurning every overture at reconciliation or intermarriage with the Mughals. The battles of Rana Pratap were fought with Rajputs on both sides of the field, for whereas large numbers of them rallied under his banner, an equally large number fought for the Mughals. Pratap's inflexible will to survive and remain unconquered touched even the heart of the enemy, and moved one of the Mughal nobles to write a poem lauding the rana's efforts. On the banks of the Pichola Lake, Rana Pratap constructed a few huts which later became the city of Udaipur.

His son, Rana Umra Singh, after some resistance yielded to the Mughals, and Jahangir, as a gesture of appreciation to the valorous enemy, commanded his son, who had defeated the rana, to place the heir of Mewar above the princes of his own house. Nevertheless, until their final domination by the British, the ranas of Mewar continued to create trouble for the imperial dynasty.

The rugged individuality of the Mewar rulers is reflected in the painting of the area, which maintained the Jain tradition long after it had disappeared elsewhere. Brilliant colors such as lacquer red, saffron yellow and lapis-lazuli, combined with angular lines of drawing, remain the outstanding characteristics of the painting of the area to the end of the seventeenth century. The crimson base of Mewar painting has its origin in the color of the Mewar flag.

Backgrounds are in monochrome or are patches of bright color against which the incidents are set, highlighting the figures and separating each group of incidents from the next. The background is stylized and the perspective extremely elementary, but quite often the treatment of trees is naturalistic in the Mughal manner. Sprays of flowers from trees and plants are common. Water is depicted by wavy lines, while trees and animals are often stylized. Horses and elephants, though, are usually treated in a realistic manner. Architecture is simple, consisting mainly of domed pavilions and turreted parapets.

Men and women both have strong, solid bodies, pronounced noses and fish-shaped eyes, imparting a fierce individuality to the face. Women lack sensuous grace, but manage to look attractive in their own way. They wear plain or flowered skirts, bodices and scarves, and their wrists are decorated with the black pompoms and tassels so often found in Pahari and Rajput pictures. It has not been established whether the pompoms had any other significance than mere decoration.

The men usually wear the *jama* with the plain, full skirt. The sash is long and decorated in geometric patterns in the fashion of the Akbar period. Quite often the pointed *jama* makes an appearance. The turban is either loosely wound or has a sash tied tightly around it. Shading of the armpit continues here long after it was discarded by the Mughals.

The painter usually depicted the Krishna legend, or mythological or historical subjects. No portraits seem to have been painted. Eighteenth-century miniatures show a greater tendency toward ornamentation. The primitive quality of earlier painting gives way, under increasing Mughal influence, to a delicacy of drawing, a fineness of line and a general blending in of colors. However, a naive quality is always discernible, especially in the use of perspective. Since the primary concern is design, realism did not seem to concern the artist. But this trait, of course, he shares with his Rajput counterparts.

The decline of the school follows the classical pattern of other schools. There is a loss of vitality, harshness of color and crudity of line. With the decline of technique, later pictures show portraits, harem scenes, processions and hunting scenes. One even finds studies of favorite horses and elephants.

JAIPUR

The first seat of power in this state was Amber, situated about six miles from the city of Jaipur. Its ruler was the first of the Rajput princes to pay homage to Babar. His son, Bhagwandas, a friend of Akbar, gave the latter his daughter in marriage, and she became the mother of Prince Salim, who later became Emperor Jahangir.

Man Singh, nephew and successor of Bhagwandas, was one of the most powerful nobles at the court of Akbar. It was due to his military skills that vast areas were annexed by the Mughal empire. Jai Singh, who was given the title "Mirza Raja," prince-king, by Jahangir, was a general in Aurangzeb's time. It was he who captured the redoubtable Shivaji and brought him to the court a prisoner. His later namesake, Sawai Jai Singh, founded the present city of Jaipur, the first planned city of India in historical times, with streets intersecting at right angles. To the love of art displayed by his forebears, Jai Singh II brought a love of science. It was from instruments of his own invention that he erected observatories at Delhi, Jaipur, Ujjain, Banaras and Mathura. The size of the observatories and the surprisingly correct results yielded by them astound scientists even now.

The close friendship between this Rajput state and the Mughals and the constant traffic to and fro made it inevitable for Jaipur painting to follow the Mughal pattern. If examined closely, however, the differences are quite marked. The delicately rounded Mughal female face gives way in Jaipur painting to a decidedly oval shape with a sharp nose. Fashions are also different. The tight pyjamas worn by the Mughal lady under her transparent gown were replaced by the typical Rajasthani dress consisting of a skirt, a tight bodice and a scarf. Some figures with Mughal features and sporting Mughal costumes give an indication of great freedom of travel between the two areas. Later, the Mughal costume completely disappears. The use of jewelry and makeup becomes excessive and the eyes, though not as large as in Jain or Mewar works, become very pronounced with the outer edges slightly upturned. The accentuated stiffness of the hems of the skirts of both men and women became a characteristic seen in late Jaipur painting.

The Jaipur miniature is simpler in composition than its Mughal counterpart, and shows a lack of depth in both outline and color treatment. The setting off of the figures by color contrast is as much a Jaipur characteristic as a feature of other Rajput schools.

In addition to religious subjects, Jaipur miniatures depict scenes of pleasure and amorous dalliance—not only between men and women but between women also. Apparently, the virile character of the court soon degenerated, and indoor rather than outdoor activities became the norm. This is reflected by the absence of scenes of the hunt, so beloved of the Mughals.

The Schools

JODHPUR (MARWAR)

Marwar is a corruption of Maroo-war, meaning "the region of death." The bards termed it Mordhur or, when compelled by the exigencies of meter, simply Maroo. Originally, the area covered the entire desert from the river Sutlej to the Arabian Sea, and was ruled by the Rathors, a Rajput clan. In A.D. 470, Nain Pal conquered Kannauj, the capital, and the dynasty was known as Kannaujia Rathor. In the twelfth century one of the nephews of the ruler, Jai Chand, set up an independent kingdom in the desert. This soon spread, and by the sixteenth century the whole desert area was studded with forts. It is estimated that at any time 50,000 members of the clan could take the field against the imperial army of Delhi.

Jodhpur was founded by Rao Joda in 1459, and replaced Mundore as capital. In 1569 Raja Maldeo of Jodhpur was defeated, and he sent his son Chandra Sen to Akbar. The latter, however, was dissatisfied with the raja's refusal to pay homage himself and laid siege to the fort, which could not hold out for long. Udai Singh, the raja's older son, later became one of Akbar's generals and was shortly after invested with the title "Mota Raja," or "Fat King," either as a gesture of humor or affection. Joda Bai, a princess of Jodhpur, became one of Akbar's wives, and the emperor restored to Marwar almost all the territory he had wrested from it and added more.

Since most of the old Jain temples are situated in Marwar, the area may have served as the center of a modified form of Gujarati art in the fifteenth century. When the Mughal style of art reached the area, it was combined with Rajput sentiment and Jain composition, resulting in a school of its own. By the middle of the seventeenth century, the Mughal style had been adopted in Jodhpur and the main characteristics of the school began to emerge. The picture became larger, about three feet square, the drawing heavier, the figures more buxom, the costumes more elaborate and the colors warmer.

Jodhpur faces are always drawn in profile and the people depicted have small heads with very high, rounded foreheads, elongated eyes turning up at the outer corners in the case of women, and slightly hooked noses. Women are long-legged, with rounded bosoms and buttocks and small waists.

The Mewar characteristic of projecting the figures against patches of color continues here, and the same colors—brilliant reds, yellows, ultramarines and oranges are found in seventeenth-century miniatures. By the mid-eighteenth century, however, these had become considerably more toned down and subtle. Gradually the drawing became exaggerated, and coats and skirts stood out like bells. Figures lost their correct proportions, the heads became too big and the legs very squat. Men's turbans become funnel-shaped and extremely high. Chunky jewelry, done in blobs of paint to give a three-dimensional effect, deck human figures and horses in the nineteenth century. By this time, scenes of revelry and the harem became predominant and were interspersed with occasional hunting scenes.

BIKANER

The state of Bikaner was formed in the fifteenth century by Beeka, son of Joda, who founded Jodhpur. The capital was founded in April-May of 1489. One of Beeka's descendants, Rai Singh, was related to Akbar through his wife, whose sister was married to Akbar. This gave the raja influence at the Mughal court, and he was given territory taken from an erring ruler. His successors remained in favor with the Mughals, and some even lost their lives fighting for the empire.

At the end of the seventeenth century, Mughal artists, the most important of whom was Ruknuddin, came to settle in Bikaner. Hindu and Muslim elements were combined in a marriage of Mughal naturalism and Rajput exuberance and love of color. In certain miniatures the colors adhere closely to those used by the Mughals: they are somber and subtle, imbuing the picture with a majestic significance. Others are brightly colored, though not with the primary colors used by Mewar artists, and more vivid than those seen at Delhi and Agra. Figures tend to be elongated and men sport the distinctive Bikaner turban. Sport seems to have been a common pastime, and hawks were carried as emblems of gentility and affluence. Pictures of hawks preying on birds of various kinds watched by the raja and his retinue were very popular.

Bikaner painting closely resembles the Jodhpur style, especially in the high-stepping quality of horses and in clothes. There is a great similarity in facial features also, as Bikaner foreheads are as rounded as those of Jodhpur, though the noses are not as hooked.

The top of the picture features a deep perspective, with people, elephants, horses, houses and trees. Flattened hillsides with a row of modeled trees are Bikaner characteristics.

The Schools

BUNDI

Bundi is bordered on the north by Jaipur and on the west by Mewar. It refused to submit to Mewar authority, and as a result the rana of Mewar besieged the fort, only to be repulsed. Peace was made later, and Bundi fought with Mewar against the Mughals until Rao Surjan (1554–85) gave up Mewar vassalage in order to become subject to the Mughals, for Akbar offered him magnanimous terms after the siege of Ranthambhar. He was made a general in the Mughal army and received great honors. His grandson Rao Rattan Singh (1607–31) pleased Jahangir, who conferred high titles on him. During his reign contacts were established with the Deccan courts, accounting for the definite Deccan influence in Bundi painting.

Shah Jahan endowed Madhav Singh, brother of the ruler Satrusal (1631–56), with land which included Kota. Satrusal had painters in his employ and soon Kota also became an important center of painting. As the Mughal empire broke up, the struggle for supremacy among the Rajput states intensified. Raja Jai Singh II (also known as Sawai Jai Singh) of Jaipur wanted to annex Bundi, and in the ensuing struggle Bundi lost part of its territory. Raja Bheem Singh of Kota seized all Bundi territory east of the river Chambal, thus impoverishing the state.

In 1719 the ruler of Kota attacked Bundi and forced its ruler, Buddha Singh, to flee. The latter's son, Ummed Singh, was able to return to Bundi in 1784 only with Maratha help. Maratha influence continued to be felt in Bundi and Kota until the states came under British protection in the following century.

Bundi painting, therefore, shows all these influences. There is the Mewar influence in the long, oval shape of the eyes, the Mughal in the rounded female face and male costumes, and the Deccan influence in certain facial types and the treatment of landscape. The placing of the pavilion, a Deccan characteristic, forms an important part in the composition of Bundi pictures.

The Bundi school of miniature painting came into full flower in the eighteenth century, although there is little doubt that painting had flourished in the area earlier. The school shows vigorous Mewar influence and that of the highly refined Mughal school. It is distinguished by lush landscapes that reflect the terrain of the state and by vibrant colors. Water is indicated in swirling eddies by means of white lines drawn on a dark gray background. A lotus pond filled with lotus, fish and birds is a favorite with the Bundi artist. The green tone of the trees is enlivened with white, red and yellow flowers, and spiked flowering plants give a most decorative look to the picture. A row of trees at the top of the picture is a common Bundi characteristic.

In seventeenth-century Bundi miniatures, Mewar influence is visible in the clothes and in the technique of depicting Krishna and his companions against a lacquer red background. The Mughal influence is noticeable in the patterns on women's skirts, the shading, the more delicate colors in the background and in the flowering shrubs, and the realism and animation of the scenes. The treatment of the female face and figure is Mewar, but the draftsmanship is much more refined and the faces more delicate.

Bundi women have small, round faces with thrusting noses and slightly receding chins. Contrary to the Mewar technique of drawing flat faces, Bundi faces are given depth and roundness with shading on the cheeks and near the eyes and nose. The color of the face is a distinct red. Late seventeenth-century women are tall and slight, with slender waists.

The female dress consists of colored or patterned pyjamas and bodice, over which a transparent *jama* with a deep, frilled V-neck is sometimes worn. Sometimes a skirt is worn instead of the pyjamas. A fine scarf is tucked into the waist of the skirt and pulled over the back of the head and the shoulder and allowed to hang down the back. A decorative sash hangs down the front. In the first half of the eighteenth century, the bosom is left exposed, but later it is covered by drawing the scarf over the bosom and under the arm on the left much in the way the saree is draped.

Male dress is very similar to the Mughal style, with the decorated sash of the Shah Jahan period. The turban is cylindrical in appearance, with a crossband pulled over the forehead, one end pointing up in a fanlike manner. Shading in the armpit region is present as in earlier Mughal painting.

The decline of the school in the eighteenth century is marked by harsher colors, cruder lines and less distinct techniques. The reddish brown tones of the face are now replaced by bright pink, and the earlier smooth shading becomes harsh and streaky. Water is depicted by heavier lines, and plain backgrounds give place to heavily shaded green mounds. The sky is colored with swirling patches of red, dark blue and gold. The trend toward ornamentation is apparent in women's clothes, which are now more sumptuously decorated with gold.

The Schools

Later Bundi paintings begin to lose their main characteristics. The trees clustered together in the typical Bundi manner are now devoid of flowers, and leaves are shaded to give an illusion of depth. The brightness of the sky disappears. The face is bordered by a patch of dark color to pick it out from its surroundings. There is a porcelain quality to skin texture, which is accentuated by the use of fine, closely set delicate lines so popular with later Mughal artists. The figures are more squat and there is a general effete appearance.

Still later, colors become crude and garish and faces larger, with heavy chins and foreheads smeared with sandalwood paste.

KOTA

The rajas of Kota were an offshoot of the Bundi family. Raja Durjan Sal, who ruled between 1724 and 1810, was a valiant prince with all the Rajput attributes of generosity, bravery and chivalry. He was a great sportsman and was especially fond of tiger hunts. Vast preserves with ditches, palisades and hunting seats were found in every part of his domain.

The hunting expeditions were organized with a meticulous eye for detail, based on a war plan, and invariably included queens and princesses. The latter were well-versed in the use of firearms and shot many tigers. The raja had to give the signal to shoot before anyone could fire. On one occasion the commander of the garrison found himself eye to eye with a tiger while still at the foot of the scaffolding. Since the raja had not given the signal to fire, the commander caught the tiger as it leapt on him and laid it low with one slash of his sword. Obviously the hunt was a great favorite with the painters of this school, taking the place of the romantic episodes depicted by the other schools.

The main characteristic of Kota painting is the vibrant life with which the forest is imbued. The thick jungles surrounding the area instilled a feeling of awe in the inhabitants, an emotion that is reflected in the artist's work. The lush vegetation, the menace of the large trees and plants, through which animals roam unfettered and which totally dwarf man, impart a unique quality to Kota painting. It is strongly reminiscent of the paintings done by Douanier Rousseau in the West. The colors are dark and lush, and the presence of wild animals is reflected in the waving branches of trees and the curve of the hills in the background. There is no attempt at realism, and darting animals surrounded by writhing branches and hanging cliffs seem to be part of a dream verging on a nightmare. Restraint is provided by the hunters watching the eerie scene and waiting patiently for their chance to kill. With increased control over the environment, the jungle lost its terror. Later pictures show lighter colors and more muted surroundings. The ferocity of lions and tigers is set off by the introduction of playful monkeys, herds of deer, blooming flowers and the gentler elements of nature. By the middle of the last century, man becomes more important than the jungle.

KISHANGARH

Kishangarh lies almost in the center of Rajasthan and has both Jodhpur and Jaipur for its neighbors. It was founded in 1609 by Kishan Singh, one of the sons of the Jodhpur ruler. The city and the fortress are both situated on the Gundalao Lake, which during the winter months is a sanctuary for geese and wild fowl of all kinds. Kishan Singh, the founder, was a worshiper of Krishna as a dancer, a creed closely associated with the *bhakti* cult, which had become the mainspring of art, literature and music. His descendants, both male and female, were also ardent followers of the religion which was to have great importance for painting.

Savant Singh, his successor, also known as Nagari Das, was born in 1699. He received a good education and was well versed in Sanskrit and Persian. He also learned music and painting, becoming reasonably adept in both, but his literary and artistic pursuits did not keep him confined to the palace. He was a warrior-prince in the best tradition—at the age of ten he controlled a wild elephant, and later is said to have fought and killed a lion.

In the tradition of courts of that period he gathered together a galaxy of talent. Devotion to Krishna was an integral part of his being and throughout his life he longed for Vrindavan, Krishna's home town, a sentiment which he often expressed in verse. Indeed so great was this mystic bent that his father, Raj Singh, sensing the conflict in his son's nature pointed out that it was improper for a prince to live the simple life because pomp and pageantry were essential trappings of royalty.

The mystic side of Savant Singh's nature found a perfect object in Bani Thani, a beautiful, young slave girl brought by his mother from Delhi. A talented musician and singer, well versed in the love poetry of the Krishna legend, her devotion to the prince matched his love for her. They worshiped and sang together, the prince as enrapt in the beauty of his beloved as in his devotion to the god.

The Schools

Later fratricidal strife disgusted him so much that Savant Singh abdicated, and, followed by the faithful Bani Thani, went to Vrindavan, where they spent the rest of their days. Here Bani Thani composed verses and sang them, while her lover gazed at her and wrote "I drank with my eyes the beauty of this glamorous woman who stood near Biharilal (one of the forms of Krishna) in ecstasy."

All these factors, combined with Savant Singh's connections with the Mughal court, had a far-reaching effect on Kishangarh painting. He rallied to the cause of Farrukhsiyar, who managed to gain the throne of Delhi in 1713, and gained great favor at the latter's court. The elegance of the costumes of Farrukhsiyar's court, along with the elongation of figures which had started in the reign of Aurangzeb and continued in later reigns, affected both Kishangarh fashions and painting.

Kishangarh painting is distinguished by the fine quality of brushwork and the distinctive features of the women's faces. The inspiration for the elongated, heavy-lidded eyes, curved eyebrows, pointed nose and long neck was, of course, Bani Thani herself. In Surdhaj Nihal Chand, Savant Singh found an artist who could translate his emotions into visual form. Nihal Chand's finest works, which were done between 1735 and 1757, depict Bani Thani and Savant as Radha and Krishna.

In her image he created his ideal of womanhood: modest and elegant, embodying all the attributes of perfection. In any scene depicting a number of women we find the same face, with slight modifications, and the central figure always shows Bani Thani as Radha. It is also interesting to note the similarity of features in Krishna. The resemblance between Krishna and Radha in these paintings is remarkable. Yet, somehow, it is not the resemblance of brother and sister, but of two parts embodying the same concepts and ideas, one female and the other male.

More than any other school, Kishangarh painting is imbued with an almost palpable quality of mysticism. The two main figures always appear as a quiet island of calm. Though not necessarily in close proximity, they seem always to be linked together by a celestial rapport, completely absorbed in each other, oblivious to the activity around them.

The blazing sky, rich with sunset colors, usually forms the backdrop of this perfect companionship. The architecture is not always a representation of the city of Kishangarh, but often an idealized version of the Dwarka of Krishna's days. The lake, which is often featured, is full of birds and fish of all kinds.

Earlier Kishangarh painting showed an elongation of figures in the style of the

Mughal school of the late Aurangzeb period. Later miniatures were made in the general tradition of Rajput painting and lost the characteristic style of Nihal Chand.

THE PAHARI SCHOOLS

Pahari is the generic name for the paintings done in the various hill states of the Punjab, whose rulers were great patrons of the arts in the seventeenth and eighteenth centuries. The art of miniature painting was brought to the Punjab from the Mughal and Rajput states, and along the way it collected the traditions of both schools. As in the case with Rajput schools, the various schools that grew up in this region differed according to the states that fostered them, the most important being Basohli, Kangra, Guler, Garhwal, Jammu, Kulu, Nurpur, Chamba, Mandi and Bilaspur.

From a court art under the Mughals, miniature painting, by the time it reached the hill states, had became a vehicle for the expression of the painter's feelings and his beliefs in religion and love. The Krishna legend, with its pastoral setting and its characters, emanating from the ranks of commoners rather than the nobility, gave the artist a chance, as in Europe, to portray the milieu with which he himself was most familiar. Just as the Madonna was depicted as a Flemish or Italian peasant girl with the dress and characteristics of the area, so Krishna became a Pahari cowherd surrounded by Pahari maidens in a hill setting. This is the terrain found at the foothills of the Himalayas and not merely an idealistic setting.

A whole series of miniatures, depicting various incidents from the life of Krishna or one of the great epics, was painted in this area. These were not done in any order, but according to the fancy of the artist or his patron. Since they were not meant as book illustrations, a few lines of text on the back or margins of the picture sufficed to describe the incident depicted.

Apart from these mythological depictions, the miniature also featured portraits or pictures of girls playing ball or musical instruments or amusing themselves with birds and animals. Like the later Mughal ladies, the Pahari ladies also liked to have themselves painted bathing, letting off fireworks, playing checkers or at their toilette.

The *nayika* and *nayik* of Rajput miniatures are also found here in various moods

The Schools

of yearning, expectation or union. The heroine occupies a prominent place in the Pahari school, while the hero is relegated to a secondary position. The *dutika*, or female messenger, who carries messages between the lovers, also holds an important place and forms the third point in the triangle. The *ragamala* series, so beloved of Rajput painters, is not nearly so common in Pahari painting, although it is often featured.

Portraits of princes, either alone or with nobles, abound, and quite often copies with minor variations were made from one picture. Many rulers had their courts painted again and again and European travelers, military commanders and officials all had portraits painted by local artists. Scenes of war or political events, such as the signing of treaties and the receiving of ambassadors, are extremely rare.

The Pahari schools bear a distinct resemblance to the Mughal school of painting around the first half of the eighteenth century. Mughal fashions in dress prevailed, and the favorite Mughal background of low, rounded hillocks with small trees roughly painted on the slopes is frequently seen, as are the Mughal-style tree formations consisting of small flat circles closely grouped together. Rows of cypress trees separated by rounded trees, another Mughal touch of the same century, are a great favorite, as are banana trees, leafy trees and flowering shrubs in close proximity.

Not every work in a style attributed to an important school emanated from the place itself. During its dominance, each school influenced the surrounding areas and even regions far away. Prior to 1745 the dominant style was that of Basohli, and miniatures in the Basohli style were painted in Nurpur, Mankot, Jasrota and Guler.

Contact between the Mughals and the rulers of the hill states was on many levels. Each raja paid a fee of investiture to the emperor on his accession and in turn received gifts from the imperial court. Princes or close relations of the rajas were kept as hostages by the Mughals to ensure the loyalty of the rulers. Mughal influence, therefore, was predominant in the realms of art and architecture. The rich and progressive states noted and followed every change in fashion of the suzerain power, while the smaller and poorer states continued with the same fashions long after they had been abandoned elsewhere.

An interest in painting came to be regarded as a sign of culture, and the rajas set up ateliers, although their earliest patronage in the field seems to have been for wall painting. Many palaces had their walls decorated with frescoes, which were, in many cases, later covered with whitewash.

COLORS

Gold and silver were used for decoration on clothes, utensils, thrones, chairs and carpets. Gold was used for lightening clouds and depicting streaks of lightning. Occasionally, the whole background was painted gold, silver being used to depict water and lotuses. Since silver tarnishes, it gradually changed color and now appears as a metallic gray-black.

The spectrum of colors range from brilliant yellow, red, blue and orange to delicate pastel shades. The latter are most frequently found in Kangra and its allied schools, while the more vibrant colors are found in Basohli. As in other schools, the colors to be used were frequently written on the drawing as an aid to the artist who filled them in later.

DRESS

Cowherds are usually shown wearing fitting shorts with a sash tied around the waist. The decorated ends, with both geometrical and floral designs, hang down to the knees. The upper part of the body is bare, and a blanket is draped over the shoulders. This is often gathered along one side to make a cloak for protection against rain and cold. The headgear is a pointed cap around which a decorated sash with loose hanging ends is tied. Sometimes pyjamas are worn with a plain sash and a scarf is thrown around the shoulders.

Deities usually wear crowns—a golden jeweled circle with five points in front and two semicircular projections behind. The central point of Krishna's crown is usually ornamented with a peacock feather, while those at the sides have lotus flower decorations. When Krishna or his brother Balarama are depicted wearing conical caps like the cowherds, these, too, are ornamented with peacock feathers.

Men's fashions approximate closely to those prevailing at the Mughal court in the reigns of Shah Jahan and Aurangzeb. Turbans are often decorated with a jeweled ornament holding a plume. Rajas sometimes wear fresh flowers in their turbans, while a conical hat of Tibetan origin with upturned brim is often found in Kulu paintings. Necklaces, bracelets, armlets and anklets form part of the masculine accessories.

The Schools

Women's clothes also show Mughal fashions—tight pyjamas, a loose or tight blouse and a long, opaque or transparent overgarment fastening over the breast and reaching down to the ankles. Often attached to the waist and tucked into the pyjamas is a decorated or plain sash reaching down to the ankles. A fine or thick scarf covers the head and shoulders, its decorated ends reaching low down the back. Frequently, between the neck and breast fastenings, an oval opening is left to reveal a tantalizing glimpse of flesh. The sash, ever-present in earlier paintings, later becomes optional, and the scarf has almost the texture of a sheet. Ladies of position wear fine, patterned fabrics with gold or decorated edges, while attendants wear outfits in coarser materials.

The Kangra overgarment looks almost like a European empire-style dress, which was probably an adaptation of the Mughal fashion, whose flattering lines may have appealed to Empress Josephine of France and so influenced European fashion. Sometimes Kangra women also wear turbans.

Another type of Pahari female costume is the Rajput-style tight bodice, full skirt and scarf, the sash being optional. The bodice is considerably abbreviated, revealing the lower part of the breasts and leaving a vast expanse of flesh visible. One end of the scarf is tucked in at the waist and taken around the back, across the bosom, and draped over the shoulders and head, with the other end trailing down the back. Where the empire-style gown and the bodice and skirt is depicted in the same picture, it is interesting to note that it is always the high-born lady who wears the former, pointing to the fact that it was essentially a court fashion. In some miniatures, however, Radha, as well as her maidens, wear the bodice and skirt.

STYLE

Depending on the whim of the patron or the lavishness of a court, Pahari miniatures have either severely plain or highly ornamented backgrounds. In the latter case, one finds carpeted pavilions with mosaic work on the walls and ceilings, while striped and floral materials are used for floor coverings, bolsters, canopies and clothing. Large trees with spreading branches and thick foliage, sometimes laden with fruits, form the landscape, along with cypresses, banana trees and flowering shrubs. Often these fill practically the whole canvas, and human figures are only apportioned a small space. But this is so cunningly handled that it is the figures rather than the surroundings that form the focal point of the picture. Night scenes with star-studded skies and scenes of storms with lightning cutting through the darkness are Pahari favorites. Both the Mughal and Deccan techniques of vertical and horizontal division of space to achieve perspective are used here.

Nowhere else does the *hookah*, or water pipe, make as frequent an appearance as in the hill regions. Perhaps it is to ward off the cold more than anything else, for even today the hookah is kept well stocked with glowing coals the whole day. Every member of the family, including small children, takes an occasional puff as they go about their business. In the paintings both men and women are shown indulging their taste for it, and in certain court scenes each courtier is shown with his hookah in front of him, its long pipe draped elaborately, adding to the ornamental quality of the pictures.

BASOHLI

Basohli, situated near the right bank of the river Ravi, became the capital of Basohli State in 1630. The town is situated on a steep hill with the river at its foot. It is surrounded by high mountains, some of them snow-clad all year round. The palace, a veritable fortress, dominates the town and is, in turn, overhung by the citadel, which has been described as being "like an eagle's nest."

The ruler, Raja Krishan Pal, was defeated by the Mughal forces in 1590 and appeared at the court of Akbar soon after. The contact thus established continued, leading to the assimilation of Mughal culture in various fields. It was the ruler Kripal Pal (1678–94) who established an atelier and started the form of miniature painting in this region. Basohli was not a large state, but under Raja Sangram Pal (1635–73), it made itself a power to be reckoned with and its cultural influence dominated the hill region. Painting flourished under Kripal Pal's patronage, being used mostly to illustrate various texts. The date, provenance and the name of the artist were often mentioned in the colophon.

The fierce facial types in early Basohli painting find a natural setting in such craggy surroundings. Even a portrait of Kripal Pal is in the same style. The strongly primitive character of early Basohli painting cannot be ascribed to the lack of experienced artists. The well-known painter Devidas and others who worked in the atelier were familiar with the Mughal style as practiced under Aurangzeb. This is evidenced in the elongation of figures characteristic of the Mughal school of this period. There is also a similarity in the costumes and architecture of the two schools. The only explanation for this seems to be a desire to break away from existing conventions and to express strong passions and emotions with sharp lines and vivid colors. The old Jain influence, always in the back of the Hindu painter's mind, combined with the Rajput and Mughal styles, could have been responsible for the art as it developed in the early days of Basohli.

Early Basohli painting is marked by a vigor and vitality that is seldom met with in other schools. The primitive element is present to an almost startling degree. Figures are tall and slim, with tapering egg-shaped heads. Features are sharply defined, with a touch of fleshiness around the chin. The eye is long and well marked. It is a proud, vital face, dominated by a forehead sloping to a high hairline.

Tight pyjamas and bodices are worn by the women under long, full-sleeved overgarments which fasten on the chest up to the waist and hang to mid-calf. This sways open with every movement to reveal a full length of leg. Sash ends, beautifully decorated, fall from waist to foot, and the women's heads are covered with gauzy scarves which are draped over the bosom and hang down the back. There is a profuse use of jewelry, mostly pearls. Beetles' wings are used on the works to give a glittering appearance to the compositions.

The Basohli artist balanced the architectural features of the miniatures with expanses of open country so that there is a sense of outdoor living. A special type of pavilion in the late seventeenth and early eighteenth centuries shows the decorated heads of animals or monsters protruding from the base. Inlaid panels and goblets placed in wall niches, a Mughal touch, are another early Basohli characteristic.

The landscape is highly stylized, and forests and groves are delineated by a circle of trees occupying the main space with the figures placed within the circle. Trees look like giant dahlias with either short, thick trunks or long, narrow ones. Other trees are oval in shape, with leaves kept firmly within their outlines, while still others are a series of fine stems with a linear depiction of leaves. The weeping willow is very popular.

Basohli cattle, like the human figures, are slightly elongated, with narrow bodies, sloping hindquarters and thin, upraised necks. After the mid-eighteenth century, the heads remain the same, but the bodies and necks become much thicker.

The colors used are the same bright reds, yellows and blues of Malwa painting, highlighting the vital quality of the work.

Indian Miniatures

What we know as the "Pahari look" is a gradual development that cannot be said to have originated in any particular school at a special date. The "new look" became most evident in the female form, although male figures also underwent a change. By about 1775 we find the emergence of a new type of female figure: there is a fragile delicacy to the frame and a porcelain quality to the women's faces. The eyes became narrower and the lips curved in the suggestion of a smile. The whole stance is one of modesty and pliability. In keeping with this new-found modesty, women's clothes covered the entire form, with only the suggestion of a bosom. The head is decorously covered and the hair falls in soft lines on the shoulders.

The primitive form of Basohli painting was gradually replaced by this new look. As time progressed, paintings acquired an artificial and frozen look. Outlines lost their flowing characteristics and faces their eager vitality. The figures became slightly distorted, with a disproportionate placing of the waist and a stumpy neck.

For some time Basohli painting, in spite of the rounded urban look it acquired, continued to retain its individuality through the long, protruding eye. By the late eighteenth century, however, Basohli art became indistinguishable from that of the other Pahari schools. Some of the pictures have been attributed to Basohli after this period mainly because they were found there or because of some detail, such as a special landmark, rather than any distinguishing feature.

KANGRA

Kangra is a large state, eighty miles long and thirty-five miles wide, bounded by Chamba, Guler and Mandi. The mountains rise sharply to the north of the area, soaring to heights of 13,000 feet. The valleys are irrigated by streams from the rivers Beas and Ban Ganga, and are richly cultivated and full of fruit trees.

The dynasty is immensely old, predating the *Mahabharata* epic. During the Akbar era, the state was ruled by Raja Bidhi Chand (1585–1605), acting as regent for his father, Jai Chand, who had been captured by Akbar during the revolt of the Punjab against Akbar in 1588. Jai Chand sent his son, Tirlok Chand, to the Mughal court as hostage, and the latter grew up with Jahangir but incurred his hostility by refusing to part with his pet parrot. Jahangir is believed to have invaded Kangra some years later and to have killed Tirlok Chand. Kangra was permanently ruled by a Mughal governor and his garrison, and Kangra rulers continued guerrilla wars against the Mughals. By Aurangzeb's time peace had been restored, and Vijairam Chand (1660–87) was invested with the *jagir* by Aurangzeb. His nephew succeeded him and was also favored by the emperor.

Mughal artists came to Kangra after the invasion of India by Nadir Shah of Persia in 1739, and were followed by others in increasing numbers. Kangra painting blossomed under Sansar Chand, who came to the throne in 1775 at the age of nine. By the time he was twenty-one, his position was secured by skillfully winning back a valuable part of his territory which had been taken by the Sikhs. He is described by a historian as generous and kind to his subjects. "Crowds of people of skill and talent, professional soldiers and others resorted to Kangra, and gained happiness from his gifts and favors."

William Moorecroft states, "Sansar Chand has a taste for the arts (which) would have been magnificent had he possessed the means, and is more generous than suits his finances. Although his liberality is occasionally shaded by efforts of parsimony . . . he is fond of drawings, keeps several artists who execute the minute parts with great fidelity but are almost wholly ignorant of perspective. His collection of drawings is very large."

In 1806–8, the Gurkhas invaded Kangra State, devastating the countryside and forcing Sansar Chand to yield considerable territory. His last years were spent in decadent pursuits, but he never lost his love for the arts and continued to patronize artists. It was thanks to his efforts that Kangra became the most famous name in Pahari painting. The style became predominant in the whole area, influencing every state and every school of painting in the region. It is not clear where the style originated, but the Kangra female beauty remained unrivaled outside the state, although it was frequently copied elsewhere. It has become common now to call that style of painting, characterized not only by the definite shape of features but also by its dreamy quality, as the Kangra style or Kangra Kalam. The late Mughal style practiced in the area before the emergence of the Kangra style is referred to as pre-Kangra.

The Kangra face is distinguished by a straight nose, almost in line with the forehead, narrow, curved eyes and delicate modeling. The hair is carefully executed and falls in a well-ordered cascade down the back. Here is the epitomy of femininity, where every action is pervaded by a sense of modesty. This quality is always present, even in rather improbable situations, such as explicit scenes of love-making or bathing in the nude.

A slightly altered face is found in miniatures of a lesser aesthetic excellence or miniatures painted at a later date. Here the nose is a bit too straight and the face projects a little too far from the neck. There is little attempt at modeling, specially where chin and throat are concerned. The delicacy is completely missing. The hair is just a black mass with very little brushwork. The Kangra artist seems to have had considerable difficulty in depicting the eyes in a frontal view. They are usually slightly out of alignment, thus giving the subject a piquantly cross-eyed look.

The Kangra landscape is naturalistic, being that of the area itself. But only the sylvan and gentler aspects of nature appear; the harsher aspects, such as the towering snow-covered mountains, are seldom ever met with. The cattle also approximate closely to cattle generally found in the area. They have large, heavy bodies, with ample hindquarters and short necks, and a placid appearance, quite unlike the high-stepping, almost deerlike look of their Basohli counterparts.

Cranes and other birds, snakes, deer, clouds, sunset and lightning are all favorite Pahari and, especially, Kangra characteristics. The curtain rolled up above the door is another well-liked device borrowed from Mughal painting.

Yellow, orange, green, pink, mauve, gray and white are colors used by the Kangra artist. The borders of paintings are both plain (only red, yellow or blue are used) or decorated. In decorated borders dark blue and gold are favorite combinations, while white and colored flowers, the acanthus and birds are all decorative devices. The oval frame with corner spandrels become increasingly popular in the nineteenth century. Here falcons and partridges attacking their prey are represented in cartouches interspersed with floral designs. Also shown are Shiva, Parvati and their devotees, a girl reclining on a bed and other designs.

Careful brushwork is found in the depiction of utensils, jewelry, furniture, designs of carpets and bolsters, patterns on materials and architectural details. The garments of people of status are fine of texture and beautifully decorated, while attendants and people of lower standing wear coarse materials with plainer designs. The same feudalistic concept is seen in the depiction of human figures. It is quite usual to find well-proportioned men and women along with squat and ungainly ones, a characteristic borrowed from Rajput painting.

The Schools

The obvious explanation for this would be that the painting was a composite work done by different artists of varying skills. But given the generally high quality of the painting this argument does not hold water. This unevenness can be attributed to the desire of the artist to show up the elegance of important persons and, by contrast, the lowly status of others.

Kangra painting, more than that of any other school, is imbued with a dream-like quality. The world depicted here has been referred to as the dreamland of the hills. It is strongly reminiscent of Fragonard and Watteau, the highly romantic painters of the West. This quality, found to some extent in other Pahari schools, is never present so strongly as in Kangra.

GULER

Guler is a small state bounded by Kangra and Nurpur. The word *guler* is a corruption of *gwalia* ("cowherd"). It was an unfortunate cowherd who pointed out the spot where a tiger and a goat drank from the same pool—a most auspicious place for a capital—to Raja Hari Chand (1612–27). The raja constructed a fort on the spot and called it Haripur. The cowherd had his head cut off and buried in the foundations of the fort to ensure its strength and stability.

Haripur has a semicircle of low, smooth hills on one side and a turbulent river, the Ban Ganga, set in a ravine, on the other. Huge trees abound in the area. From the fort, which is now in ruins, the Ban Ganga can be seen flowing to join the river Beas.

Migration to the hills commenced from around 1740, and some reputed artists went to work in Guler. Raja Govardhan Chand (1745–73) was a great patron of painting, and a great deal of work was done during his regime. He married a Basohli princess, and gave his own sister in marriage to his brother-in-law so that Basohli and Guler influences were intermingled.

His son, Prakash Chand (1773–90), continued the tradition. He had a vast capacity for spending large sums of money which put him in the hands of money-lenders. Like Balwant Singh of Jammu, he was very fond of having himself painted in all sorts of situations, including a picture of himself with his chief creditor, the Brahmin Avatara. He became slightly crazed and retired from public affairs in 1790, when his son, Bhup Singh, became the *de facto* raja, formally ascending the throne at his father's death.

As in Kishangarh so in Guler the special features of the ruler became the distinguishing mark of the painting of the area. Prakash Chand's slightly tilted chin became a hallmark of Guler work. The Guler turban is really a piece of cloth tied over a helmet, whose tip shows through. *Jama* are long and the sashes thick, being either plain or striped but not really ornamented.

The other characteristics of this school are a flat background with flowering shrubs and formal gardens in the foreground, large expanses of chocolate brown or red in the background, plantain trees, cypresses and rounded hills with wooded ridges.

Since the Kangra style was all-pervasive in the hill region, it is not easy to distinguish between the painting of Guler and Kangra, or any other place with the same style, but certain characteristics do help to tell the different schools apart. The face of the Guler female is more naturalistic and less idealized than that of Kangra. The eyebrows are thicker, the nose more pronounced though not longer, and the cheeks more rounded. It is the face of one who has opinions and views of her own and who is not afraid to state them.

On the whole, the Guler miniature lacks the extreme romanticism of the Kangra school of painting and is a more straightforward statement of reality.

GARHWAL

Garhwal is a large state bounded by the Punjab plain and the state of Uttar Pradesh. Until 1815 the capital was Srinagar; then the eastern and southeastern regions became the British district of Garhwal and the western and northwestern areas became the state of Tehri Garhwal, with its capital at Tehri.

Although one of the largest states in the Punjab hills, it was also one of the poorest, so much so that no tribute was levied on it by the Mughals. Akbar was told that Garhwal was like "a lean camel—up and down and very poor." In spite of its poverty, however, it was connected by marriage to Guler and Nurpur, which accounted for the influence of the two schools on Garhwal painting.

Sulaiman Shikoh, a nephew of Aurangzeb, fled from his uncle's wrath and found refuge at the court of Prithipat Shah (1638–60) of Garhwal. As was usual in those days, he came with a whole retinue, including two artists, father and son, Sham Das and Har Das. After only a year, however, the prince was handed over to his uncle by Medini Shah, the son of Prithipat Shah, presumably out of fear of incurring imperial wrath. The prince left, but the artists were allowed to stay on and work in Garhwal and were treated with favor by the ruler and his son, who were patrons of art, although Garhwal painting at this time was extremely elementary. Har Das's grandson, Molaram, became both poet and painter, and apart from writing the history of the rajas of Garhwal in Hindi verse, was an outstanding painter of the Garhwal school.

Here again one is forced to look for distinguishing features, none of which can be said to belong exclusively to the school, but, taken together, can help decide the provenance of a miniature. Although this feature is met with in other schools also, Garhwal painting shows extensive use of leafless trees and shrubs. Fan-shaped trees and shrubs with flowering spikes are also Garhwal characteristics. Lavender mauve is a favorite color, together with white.

The women's faces lack the extreme delicacy of Kangra art. The nose does not curve out from the forehead but projects from the dip where the nose and the forehead meet. A large head covered with a mass of hair, which is seen in very few other places, can help to establish a picture as belonging to Garhwal. The sandalwood paste mark worn in the shape of a crescent on the forehead, if not exclusive to Garhwal, was much favored here.

Architecture in the background is sharply defined and appears almost three-dimensional. Water is depicted by curly scroll-like ripples, while in a rainswept landscape, the falling water is depicted by a series of white parallel lines, extremely thick, forming a sort of curtain to veil the background. Lightning is depicted horizontally, covering the sky from end to end in a continuous thin curly streak.

One interesting detail marks the Garhwal miniature. When a double lotus motif appears on a pillar, the lower part of the flower has the usual proportions but the upper part has much longer petals. These are closed tightly at the bottom and unfold rather stiffly at the top.

JAMMU

Jammu, now part of the state of Jammu and Kashmir, borders on the Punjab plain and stands on the right bank of the river Tawi where it leaves the low hills. The whole area is covered with hills, and is full of shrubs and scrawny trees, as shown in the miniatures of the area. The invasion of India by Nadir Shah in 1739, and Ahmed Shah Durrani in 1752, led to the emergence of Jammu as the leading power in the Jammu hills. The town became a wealthy trade center, owing to the influx of traders and artisans from the Punjab, which had been annexed by the Afghans.

The widow of the last Mughal governor of Lahore, Mir Mannu, came and settled in the area, bringing with her painters, artisans and courtiers. Other Mughals also flocked to the area, whose Hindu rulers were noted for their religious tolerance. It was under Ranjit Dev (1735–81) and his younger brother, Balwant Singh (1724–63), that painting received real patronage. The latter used the art of portraiture lavishly, converting it into a vehicle for developing a personality cult. He had himself portrayed in every way—dictating a letter, sleeping, being shaved and even rolled up in a blanket with his favorite wife. There are also regal portraits showing him seated on his throne, holding a durbar, indulging in lion hunts and killing a tiger single-handed. There are also portraits of his favorite hawks, horses and elephants.

All these were painted by Nainsukh, who migrated to Jammu, presumably from Guler. It is not certain when Nainsukh was born or where he received his training or even when he came to Jammu. However, it is clear that his whole family was talented and traveled from Guler, where it was based, to different states. Manku, the elder brother, and his son, Fattu, worked in Basohli, while another son, Khushala, went to Kangra. Nainsukh's own sons, Gaudhu, Nikka and Ranjha worked at Kangra, Chamba and Basohli. Nainsukh himself left Jammu after the death of his patron and went to Basohli, where he died in 1778. The fact that he was a master of the painting techniques of both the Mughal and Guler courts is evident from the quality of his works. This knowledge, combined with a natural flair for portraiture and a mastery of drawing, was responsible for the skillfully executed works showing Balwant Singh at work and play.

There is an air of austerity about the paintings of this area. The lush foliage of Kangra is entirely absent and so is the dreamy romantic theme. In miniatures dating from the nineteenth century, the Sikh look predominates, and the *jama* is no longer flowing but shorter and often tucked up around the waist to allow for freedom of movement. Short-sleeved jackets are worn over long-sleeved jackets and knee-length skirts. The sash hangs down the front to the left of the waist and almost down to the knees at the back, forming a sort of girdle. This type of sash is sometimes tied over the *jama*. A sort of cloth helmet flowing down the back of the head is worn. This had the effect of flattening the top of the head and was probably used to hide the long hair of Sikh males before it became fashionable to put it into a bun at the top of the head. In later pictures the turban is styled to cover the hair on top of the head. The faces shown are those of modern Sikhs and the style is very European.

Female figures have aquiline features with highly arched eyebrows. They have the same long-legged look as the males and lack the pliant modesty of the Kangra women, having a much more assertive appearance. The skirt of the *jama* is quite often pulled back to reveal pyjama-clad legs.

Late nineteenth-century miniatures are very heavily ornamented, and a lavish use of gold and bright colors dominate. The male figure is, like most Pahari pictures, shown leaning against a bolster. In Jammu there is a profusion of flowered and patterned cushions and bolsters. One characteristic of this school is the placing of the attendant in such a way that one of his legs is covered by the bolster.

The balustrade is divided into compartments, with a knob placed over each, or each alternate, pillar. The extremely pale sky is an important charateristic and serves to divide the picture into two horizontal planes. Other characteristics are the gray background, white *jama*, and huge bolsters and cushions with floral designs. In portraits the head is drawn much larger and is disproportionate to the rest of the body.

KULU

The Kulu valley is the Kuluta visited by the Chinese pilgrim, Hsüan Tsang in the early centuries of the Christian era. Most of the area is mountainous and uninhabitable. Villages are clustered on the lower slopes and surrounded by terraced fields and orchards of apples, apricots and walnuts. Its capital, Sultanpur, was founded in 1660.

Although there was a folk tradition of painting on birch bark from ancient times, no examples of it have been found. Miniature painting seems to have started in the valley in the reign of Pritam Singh (1767–1806). A school of art flourished in Kulu in the middle of the eighteenth century. Certain characteristics of this school place it with Basohli, but on the whole the work done at Kulu has a much greater folk element than Basohli work and lacks sophistication.

Women are depicted flat-chested and even when breasts are shown these are outlined as two circles at approximately where they should be located. Hair is either tied into a tight knot at the back near the top of the head or hangs unbound down the back. Sometimes men wear long locks with dishevelled ends hanging below the shoulder on each side of the face in front of the ears, the main portion being caught up in the turban. The top of the head is egg-shaped, as in Basohli art. Arms are thin and scraggy, and hands long and inelegant. The female nose is long and tilted up, the eyes wide open, the forehead high and the face generally unrefined. Both male and female figures are flat and devoid of modeling. Some of the women are excessively tall, but generally Kulu figures are squat and ungainly.

The bodices of the women reach the waist and have a deep frill in front. The tight pyjamas and overskirts do not appear, but the women mostly wear the *choli* and the voluminous skirt, *ghagra*, with sometimes a wide band of a different colored cloth on top of the latter. The head is covered with a veil, but one breast and sometimes the whole bosom, is exposed. Cowherds wear Tibetan-type caps. Ornamentation of the clothes is depicted with tiny spread strokes of the brush, the three-dot and four-dot pattern being a great favorite for women's clothes.

In later miniatures women wear clothes that can be seen in the area even today— full skirts, a long robe tight around the waist and open and flowing below. The veil is now attached to the head by a band, and only some hair falls down the back.

Normally the background has no color wash but consists only of the cream-tinted paper on which the miniature is painted, or a light green one. Borders are either pale brick red or dark brown. Mauve, brown, gray, yellow, pink, blue, red and green are the usual colors for the paintings.

The weeping willow, found in great profusion in the valley, and the *chir* pine form part of the landscape. Stylized pine trees and one or two birds in the background are a Kulu characteristic. Trees are often shaped like dahlias, after the Basohli tradition, and have holes gouged out in the trunks. Rain is depicted by a series of dashes at set intervals giving an impression of a bead curtain, and Chinese-style clouds at the top of the picture are frequent touches.

Perhaps because of the high incidence of goiter in the area, a great many of the people in the miniatures have bulging swellings on the neck.

NURPUR

Nurpur is a small state bounded by Chamba, Basohli and Guler. Until 1590, the capital was Pathankot, after which it became Nurpur, "city of light." Situated at the entrance to the hills and at the edge of the Punjab plain, the state played a role in seventeenth-century politics that was totally unconnected with its size or importance.

In the early years of that century the rulers were actively bound to the Mughal emperors, either in friendship or enmity. When the rebellions subsided, they were accepted with favor at the Mughal court, their transgressions quickly forgiven. Relations with Basohli and Kangra were also cordial. The break-up of the Mughal empire brought many artists to Nurpur. It had a thriving artists' colony, and one artist, Golu, was so famous that a festival in his name is celebrated even today. Gurbaksh was another renowned artist.

Mauve, pink, turquoise, blue and brown are all colors favored by Nurpur artists, although brown is most frequently seen. Figures are usually placed against a plain background of long, pointed cypresses and horizontal, pronglike clouds.

Voluminous opaque drapery on certain female figures covers everything except the faces and hands, although transparent drapery is also a Nurpur feature. Whether thick or thin, clothes stick out stiffly at the edges. Often the scarf covering the head only reaches to the shoulders. Stiff, pleated folds make a distinctive pattern. Men's clothes are distinguished by half-sleeved coats with fur collars, a Deccan characteristic copied by Nurpur painters.

Women's hair is dressed so that a thin strand curls in front of the ear. The faces lack the delicacy of Kangra faces and are much stronger, with long curving eyes. The breast is emphasized by shading and there is a deliberate show of nipples through the *choli*. Women are extremely tall and short-bodied, and when they are depicted turning around, only the upper part of the body moves, giving them a very awkward look. This is the most striking Nurpur characteristic and is not met with elsewhere.

CHAMBA

The town of Chamba, situated on the river Ravi, was named after Champavati, daughter of a tenth-century raja. The people of Chamba, particularly the women, are noted for their good looks. During the time of Akbar, the state became a Mughal fief. Most hill rulers' collections have been dispersed, but Raja Bhuri Singh of Chamba donated his entire collection to a museum in 1908. This has enabled experts to estimate the quality of painting done in this small state.

The Kangra style of painting developed in Chamba from the middle of the eighteenth century around the same time as it developed in Guler. The greater portion of the work followed the general lines of the Kangra school, but in some paintings distinct differences are seen.

The typical Chamba female is unmistakeable. The mouth is compressed with pursed lips, and the eyebrows are deeply curved. The nose and forehead dominate, the lower half of the face being less important than the upper half. The expression is prim and generally disapproving. The neck is too short and thick for the usually long body.

Backgrounds are often depicted as a series of curves covering the top of the picture. Clouds have jagged edges painted with sharp strokes, or are depicted like scrolls in a distinctly Chinese manner.

MANDI

Mandi is a large state bounded by Bilaspur, Kangra and Kulu. The hills are thickly wooded and there are many torrents, with views of snow-clad mountains. A great part of the area is covered with fields and fruit trees. A traveler has described it thus: "The approach (from Kangra) to Mandi state is a Jack-and-the-bean-stalk business. At the head of the Kangra valley the road goes straight up a mountain, and at the top you are in Mandi. A switchback ride of sixty miles, a bridge with towers and gates at each end over the Beas River, here a boiling torrent, and one is in Mandi town. The river front of Mandi is a miniature Banaras: temples, old houses, long flights of steps. The streets are steep and winding, and the market place has a medieval picturesqueness."

Isvari Sen (1788–1806) was four years old when he became ruler. Mandi was invaded by Kangra; the town was looted and heavy tribute extracted. Isvari Sen was taken to Kangra and released after twelve years, when Kangra was invaded by the Gurkhas. He married a niece of Raja Sansar Chand of Kangra.

The Kangra school developed in Mandi in the early nineteenth century. Ram Dayal, an artist of Chamba, settled and painted there. Other famous artists include Muhammadi, Sanju and Narotam.

A typical Mandi characteristic is the placing of figures within an architectural setting. Shrubs and trees are placed together, their tops creating a scalloped edge.

The Schools

Borders are curved and heavily ornamented, giving an almost framed look to the picture. Bright colored saffron robes are found in some paintings of this area.

The rulers of the state had no real taste for painting and so few stylistic features emerged, and there is very little to distinguish the products of Mandi from those of late Kangra.

BILASPUR

Bilaspur is situated on both banks of the river Sutlej. It is a small town, but the state was a feudal overlord of various tiny states and was linked by marriage to Kulu, Mandi and other kingdoms. Raja Dip Chand (1650–67) campaigned for the Mughal emperor Aurangzeb, and welcomed Mughal painters to his court.

Even though Kangra influence is very strong, the Bilaspur school has its own individuality. Bilaspur women lack the delicacy of Kangra women and are quite buxom. Men also have robust bodies with short necks and faces that jut out slightly. Men wear shorts or, in some cases, *dhotis* instead of pyjamas. The ends of the sash hang just a little above or below the knee and are decorated. The headdress is a sort of conical cap with a piece of cloth tied around the base. The cowherds carry blankets for protection against inclement weather in winter. This is gathered at one end to form a kind of cloak. Hair is worn with a long corkscrew curl trained in front of the ear on one side.

Gnarled and knotted tree trunks with grass at the roots, softly rounded hillocks and a device of little dots fringing the foliage are all Bilaspur characteristics. Red, orange, white, brown and green are favorite colors.

A love of cattle seems to have been the main characteristic of the Bilaspur artist. Nowhere do they appear in such numbers or are so painstakingly depicted as here. Their bodies are lovingly drawn and decorated with gold. The langor that pervades other Pahari schools is entirely missing and there is a sense of light-hearted activity and mischief that does not exist anywhere else. The artist probably felt most at home in this pastoral scene, for there is nothing contrived or forced, and the very spontaneous quality of the work is its main charm and distinctive feature.

Appendices

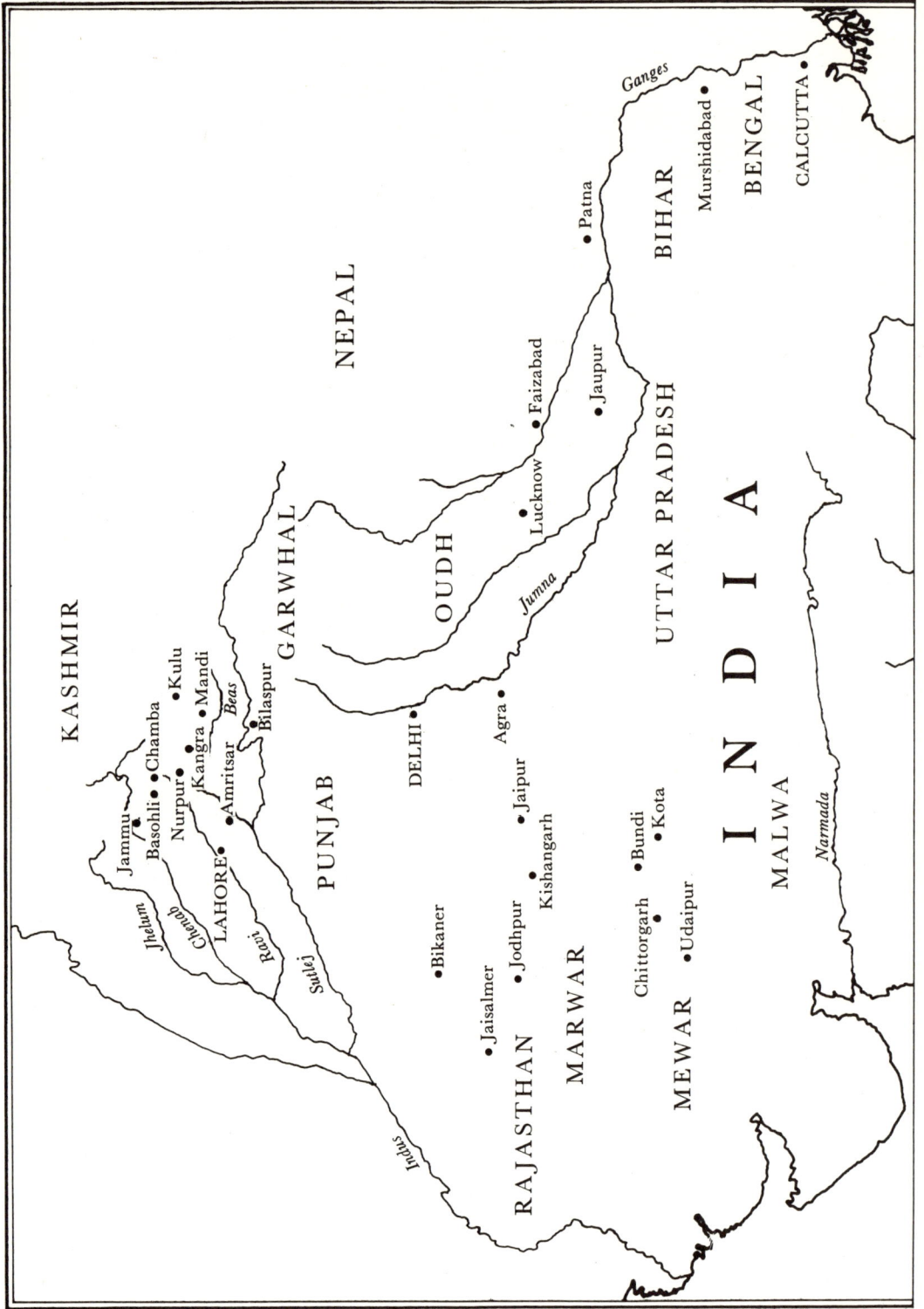

KASHMIR

Jammu

Basohli

Chamba

Nurpur

Kulu

Mandi

Kangra

Beas

Bilaspur

Amritsar

LAHORE

Jhelum

Chenab

Ravi

Sutlej

Indus

PUNJAB

GARWHAL

NEPAL

OUDH

Ganges

Murshidabad

BENGAL

CALCUTTA

BIHAR

Patna

Faizabad

Jaupur

Lucknow

Jumna

UTTAR PRADESH

DELHI

Agra

Jaipur

Kishangarh

Bikaner

Jaisalmer

Jodhpur

RAJASTHAN

MARWAR

Chittorgarh

Bundi

Kota

Udaipur

MEWAR

I N D I A

MALWA

Narmada

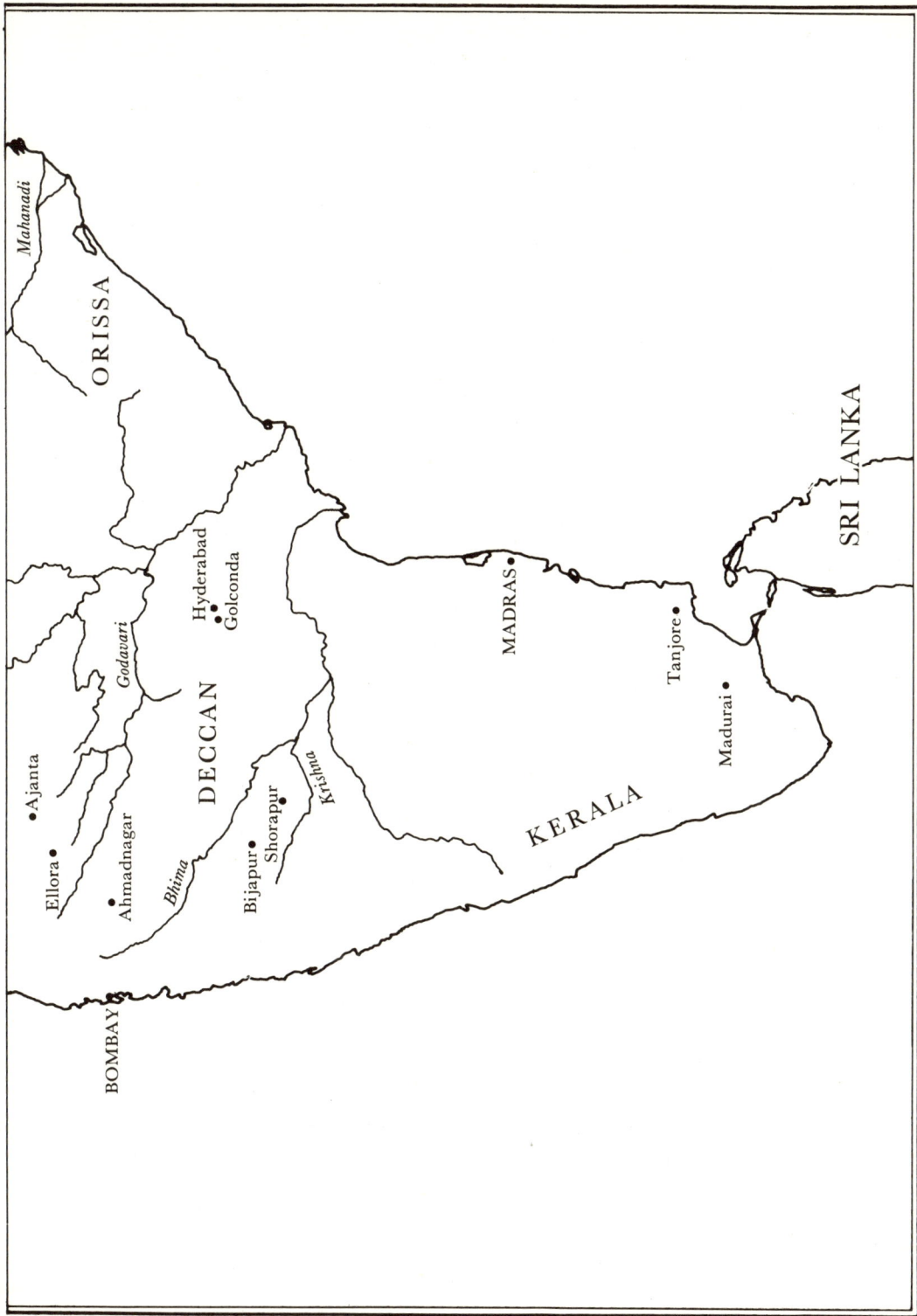

Glossary

Ab-e-rawan
Fine muslin from Dacca

Abhisandhita
Heroine who ignores her lover's devotion but misses him on separation.

Abhisarika
Heroine who braves all dangers and goes out to meet her lover

Amaltas
Cassia fistula or laburnum

Amla
Phyllanthus emblica

Amrit
Elixir of life

Anna
One-sixteenth of a rupee or a *tola* (q.v.)

Apsara
Beautiful female celestial spirit

Arhar
Cazanaus canzan

Asoka
Saraca indica

Asura
Demon or enemy of the gods

Avatar
The reincarnation of a deity

Basakasayya
Heroine who waits for her lover on the doorstep

Bhakta
Devotee

Bhang
Indian hemp

Bhayankar
Emotion of fear

Bhittichitra
Mural

Bindu
Dot

Brahmin
The highest of the four castes of the Hindus, they were priests and the repository of all learning.

Burqa
A garment that conceals the whole body with slits for the eyes

Champa
Michelia champaka

Chir
A variety of pine, *Pinus longifolia*

Chitrasala
Picture gallery

Choli
Tight bodice worn by women

Darogah
Supervisor, also a police officer
Deepa
Lamp
Dharma
Religious creed
Dhau
Anogeiss latifolia
Dharista
The hero who has neither shame nor pity
Dhoti
Thick or thin material for draping the lower half of the male body
Dhruva
A variety of aromatic grass
Dupatta
Thick or thin material for covering a woman's head, shoulders and bosom
Dutika
Female go-between

Fakir
Holy man, also a beggar

Ghagra
Voluminous skirt worn by women
Ghat
Any approach, path or steps descending to any body of water for bathing or washing clothes
Gopi
Milkmaids with whom Krishna frolicked in Gokul
Gulal
Red powder used during Holi
Gulmohar
Delonix regia
Guru
Teacher or preceptor

Harra
Terminalia chebula
Hashia
Border of a picture
Hasya rasa
Emotion of mockery
Himru
Cotton-backed satin

Jama
Coat of varying length worn by both men and women
Jatilinga
A dye made from shellac

Kachnar
Bauhinia
Kajli siyahi
Black ink
Kapittha
Elephant apple, *Seronia elephantum*
Karma
Doctrine of action, reaction and interaction
Karuna rasa
Emotion of pathos
Khandita
The heroine who scolds her lover when he fails to keep his appointment and comes to see her after spending the night with another girl
Khushnavis
Calligrapher
Kshatriya
Second highest caste, the warriors
Kundalini
Energy at the base of the spine which, if released, can lead to great spiritual excellence

Lingam
Monolith symbolizing the penis or male energy

Madder
A plant from which dye is obtained
Mahajal
Fishing nets
Maharaja
Great king
Maharani
Great queen
Manisatha
The false lover who is enraged at the rejection of his approaches.
Mirza Raja
Title bestowed on Jai I of Jaipur
Muhtasib
One who keeps accounts

Nagarika
City dweller; a cultured man
Naqsnavis
The painter of the pattern on the border of the picture
Nataraja
Shiva's cosmic dance of destruction and re-creation of the world
Nayik
Hero
Nayika
Heroine
Neem
Margosa indica
Nirvana
Supreme bliss—freedom from the cycle of rebirth
Nukhayyar
Watered paper

Pata
Long paintings on cloth that tell stories
Pati
Husband
Peshwaz
Long gown worn by women

Peori
Yellow
Prakriti
Nature or matter, prototype of the female sex
Prositapatika
Heroine whose husband is away on business
Purusha
The original eternal man

Raga
Traditional Hindu musical form or mode
Ragamala
A garland of *ragas*
Ragini
A female *raga*
Rakshasa
Goblin or evil spirit
Rani
Queen
Rishi
An inspired poet or sage
Rudra rasa
Emotion of fury

Sachchi tipai
Putting in details in a picture
Sadhu
Ascetic
Sakhi
Heroine's girlfriend
Sakti
Power or energy
Sal
Shorea robusta
Samyoga
Love in union
Sanni
Flax
Saras
A variety of crane

Glossary

Satha
The false and heartless lover
Seer
A weight equivalent to 2.18 lbs.
Siddha
Perfect or perfection
Siyahi
India ink, also darkness
Sringara rasa
Emotion of love
Subahdari
Governorship of a province under the Mughals

Tola
One-eightieth of a *seer* (q.v.)
Tipai
First sketch

Upapati
Lover

Utkanthita
The anxious heroine whose lover fails to keep his appointment

Vaisika
The accomplished seducer
Vasligar
One who mounts and frames pictures
Vedas
Earliest Indian scriptures
Vipralabdha
The disappointed heroine who waits for her lover in vain
Vira rasa
Emotion of valor

Yogi
One who undertakes a spiritual discipline, also an ascetic
Yogini
A female *yogi*

Bibliography

Agarwala, V. S. *The Romance of Himachal Paintings*. Rooplekha, AIFACS, Vol. XX, 1948–49.

Arnold, T. W., and Wilkinson, J. V. S. *The Library of A. Chester Beatty: A Catalogue of the Indian Miniatures*. 3 Vols. Oxford, 1936.

_____. *Mughal Miniatures of the Early Periods*. Oxford, 1953.

Archer, Mildred. *Patna Painting*. Royal Asia Society, London, 1948.

_____. *Indian Miniatures and Folk Paintings*. Arts Council, London, 1967.

Archer, W. G. *Indian Painting in the Punjab Hill States*. London, 1952.

_____. *Kangra Painting*. London, 1952.

_____. *Garhwal Painting*. London, 1954.

_____. *Romance and Poetry in Indian Painting*. (The Sir George Birdwood Memorial Lecture) London Journal of Royal Society of Arts, 1957.

_____. *The Loves of Krishna in Indian Painting and Poetry*. London, 1957.

_____. *India and Modern Art*. London, 1959.

_____. *Indian Miniatures*. London, 1960.

_____. *Indian Miniatures*. New York Graphic Society, 1960.

_____. *Kalighat Drawings from the Basant Kumar Birla Collection*. Bombay, 1962.

_____. *Central Indian Painting*. London.

_____. *Paintings of the Sikhs*. London, 1966.

_____. *Indian Paintings from the Punjab Hills*. London, 1973.

Banerji, Adris. *Mewar Miniatures*. Rooplekha, Vol. XXX, July 1959.

Barrett, D. E. *Painting of the Deccan*. London, 1958.

_____. *Some Unpublished Deccan Miniatures*. New Delhi, 1960.

Barrett, Douglas, and Gray, Basil. *Painting of India*. London, 1963.

Bedi, K. S., and Bal, S. S. *Essays on History, Literature, Art and Culture*. New Delhi and Chandigarh, 1970.

Binyon, L. *The Court Painters of the Grand Moguls*. London, 1921.

Blochet, E. *Les Peintures Orientales de la Collection Pozzi*. Paris, 1928.

_____. *Musulman Painting*. London, 1929.

Brown, Percy. *Indian Painting*. Calcutta, 1918.

_____. *Indian Paintings under the Moghuls*. London, 1923.

_____. *Indian Painting under the Moghals*: A.D. *1550 to* A.D. *1750*. Oxford, 1924.

Brown, W. Norman. *The Story of Kalaka: Text, History, Legends and Miniature Paintings of the Svetambara Jain Hagiographical Work the Kalakacaryakatha*. Washington, 1933.

_____. *A Descriptive and Illustrated Catalogue of Miniature Paintings of the Jaina Kalpasutra As Executed in the Early Western Indian Style*. Washington, 1934.

_____. "Some Early Rajasthani Raga Paintings." Journal of the Indian Society, of Oriental Art, Vol. XVI, 1948.

Coomaraswamy, A. K. *The Arts and Crafts of India and Ceylon*. London, 1913.

_____. "The Eight Nayikas." London Journal of Indian Art and Industry, Vol. XVI, No. 128, October 1914.

_____. *Rajput Painting*. Oxford, 1916.

_____. *Catalogue of the Indian Collection in the Museum of Fine Arts, Boston*. Boston, 1924.

Chandra, Moti. *Mewar Painting in the 17th Century*. New Delhi, 1957.

_____. "Exhibition of the Shri Moti Chand."

_____. *Mewar Painting*. New Delhi.

Chandra, Pramod. *Khajanchi Collection Held by Lalit Kala Academy 1960*. New Delhi, 1960.

_____. *Bundi Painting*. New Delhi, 1959.

Clarke, Stanley. *Indian Drawings of the School of Humayun*. London, 1921.

_____. *Indian Drawings*. London, 1922.

Dickinson, Eric, and Khandalavala, Karl. *Kishangarh Painting*. New Delhi, 1959.

Deneck, Marguerite Marie. *Indian Art*. London, 1967.

Eastman, Alvan Clark. *The Nala Damayanti Drawings: A Study of a Portfolio of Drawings Made for Raja Samsar Chand of Kangra (1774–1823)*. Boston, 1959.

Ettinghausen, Richard. *Persian Miniatures in the Bernard Berenson Collection*, Milan.

_____. *Painting of the Sultan and Emperors of India in American Collections*. New Delhi, 1961.

French, J. C. *Himalayan Art*. London, 1931.

_____. "Samsar Chand of Kangra." Journal of Indian Art and Letters, Vol. XXI, No. 2, 1947.

Gangoly, O. C. *Rajput Painting*. Calcutta, 1926.

_____. *Ragas and Raginis*. Calcutta, 1934.

Bibliography

Ghosh, Ajit. "Pahari School of Indian Painting." Rooplekha, Vol. XXVIII, March 1958.

Goetz, Herman. "Indian Painting in the Muslim Period." Journal of Indian Society of Oriental Art, Vol. XV, 1947.

_____. *Art and Architecture of Bikaner State.* Oxford, 1950.

_____. "Indian Art in the Baroda Museum." Rooplekha, Vol. XX, 1948–49.

_____. *India: Five Thousand Years of Indian Art.* Art of the World Series. Bombay, 1959 and 1960.

Gray, Basil. *Persian Painting: from Miniatures of the XIII-XVI Centuries.* London, 1945.

_____. *Treasures of Indian Miniatures in the Bikaner Palace.* Oxford, 1951.

_____. *Rajput Painting.* London.

Gupta, R. S., and Mahajan, B. D. *Ajanta, Ellora and Aurangabad Caves.* Bombay, 1962.

Havell, E. B. *Indian Sculpture and Painting,* 2nd ed. London, 1928.

Hendlay, T. H. *The Razm Namah.* Jeypore, 1893.

Hajek, Lubor. *Indian Miniatures of the Moghul School.* London, 1960.

_____. *Miniatures from the East.* London, 1960.

Kala, Satish Chandra. *Indian Miniatures in the Allahabad Museum.* Allahabad, 1961.

Kishandasa, Rai. *Mughal Miniatures.* New Delhi, 1955.

Khandalavala, Karl. *Indian Sculpture and Painting.* Bombay, 1938.

_____. "A Gita Govinda Series in the Prince of Wales Museum." Bombay, 1953–54.

_____. *Pahari Miniature Painting,* Bombay, 1958.

Khandalavala, Karl, and Moti, Chandra. "An Aviruddha-Usha Series from Chamba and the Painter Ram Lal." New Delhi, 1955–56.

_____. *The Rasa Manjari in Basohli Painting.* New Delhi, April 1956–March 1957.

_____. *Miniatures and Sculptures from the Collection of the Late Sir Cowasji Jahangir.* Bombay, 1965.

Kramrisch, Stella. *The Vishnodharmottara: A Treatise on Indian Painting.* Calcutta, 1924.

_____. *A Survey of Painting in the Deccan.* London, 1937.

Kuhnel, E, and Goetz, H. *Indian Book Painting from Jahangir's Album.* London, 1925.

Lal, Mukandi. "Garhwal School of Painting." Rooplekha, Vol. XX, 1948–49.

_____. *Garhwal Painting.* New Delhi, 1968.

Lawrence, George. *Indian Art: Paintings of the Himalayan States.* London, 1963.

Lee, Sherman E. *A History of Far Eastern Art.* London, 1964.

_____. *Rajput Painting with an Introductory Essay and Catalogue Notes.* New York.

Maclagan, Sir Edward. *The Jesuits and the Great Mogul.* London, 1932.

Mahler, Jane Gaston. *Oriental Miniatures: Persian, Indian and Turkish.* London, 1965.

Marek, J., Knizkova, H. (Olga Kuthanova, translator). *The Jenghiz Khan Miniatures from the Court of Akbar the Great.* London, 1963.

Mazumdar, R. C., Raychaudhuri, H. C., Datta, Kalikinkar. *An Advanced History of India.* London, 1950.

Bibliography

Mehta, Nanalal Chamanlal. *Studies in Indian Painting*. Bombay, 1926.

_____. *Gujarati Painting in the Fifteenth Century: A Further Essay on Vasanta Vilasa*. London, 1931.

_____. "Some Notes on Pahari Paintings." Rooplekha, Vol. XX, 1948–49.

Morand, Paul. *Chefs d'Oeuvres de la Miniature Persane: XIII-XVI Siècle*. Paris, 1940.

Nawab, Sarabhai Manilal. *The Oldest Rajasthani Paintings from Jain Bhandars*. Ahmedabad.

_____. *Masterpieces of the Kalpasutra Paintings*. Ahmedabad, 1956.

Randhawa, M. S. *Kangra Valley Painting*. New Delhi, 1954.

_____. "A Journey to Basohli." Rooplekha, Vol. XXVIII, March 1958.

_____. "Kangra Ragamala Paintings." Rooplekha, Vol. XXIX, December 1958.

_____. "Some Inscribed Pahari Paintings with Names of Artists." Rooplekha, Vol. XXX, July 1959.

_____. *Basohli Painting*. New Delhi, 1959.

_____. *Kangra Paintings on Love*. New Delhi, 1962.

Randhawa, M. S., and Archer, W. G. *Kangra Paintings of the Gita Govinda*. New Delhi National Museum, 1962.

Randhawa, M. S., and Galbraith, J. K. *Indian Painting: The Scene, Themes and Legends*. Boston and London, 1968.

Rawson, Philip. *Indian Painting*. New York, 1961.

Ray, Sudhansu Kumar. *The Ritual Art of the Bratas of Bengal*. Calcutta, 1961.

Reiff, Robert. *Indian Miniatures: The Rajput Painters*. Rutland and Tokyo, 1959.

Robinson, B. W. *Persian Paintings*. London, 1952.

Shukla, Dr. D. N. *Vastu–Sastra V: Hindu Canons of Iconography and Painting*. Lucknow.

_____. *Royal Arts: Yantras and Chitras*. Lucknow, 1967.

Singh, Kumar Sangram. *An Early Ragamala Manuscript from Pali: The Marwar School, dated A.D. 1623*. New Delhi, 1960.

Singh, Madanjeet. *The Cave Paintings of Ajanta*. London, 1965.

Sinha, R. P. N. *Geeta Govinda in Basohli School of Indian Painting*. New Delhi and Calcutta, 1958.

Sivaramamurthi, S. *South Indian Paintings*. New Delhi, 1968.

Skelton, Robert. "The Nimat Namah: A Landmark in Malwa Painting." Marg, Vol. XII, No. 3, 1959.

_____. "The Tod Collection of Rajasthani Paintings." Rooplekha, Vol. XXX, July 1959.

_____. *Indian Miniatures from the XVth to XIXth Centuries*. Venice, 1961.

Solomon, W. E. Gladstone. *Essays on Mogul Art*. London, 1932.

Stchoukine, Ivan. *Miniatures Indiennes du Mussée du Louvre*. Paris, 1929.

_____. *La Peinture Indienne à l'Epoque des Grands Moghols*. Paris, 1929.

Bibliography

Stooke, Herbert J., and Khandalavala, Karl. *The Laud Ragamala Miniatures: A Study in Indian Painting and Music.* Oxford, 1953.

Suleiman, Hamid. *Miniatures of Babur Nama: Academy of Sciences of the Uzbek S.S.R. and Ilisher Navoi Literature Museum.* Fan Publishing House of the Uzbek S.S.R. Tashkent, 1970.

Todd, James. *Annals and Antiquities of Rajasthan.* London, 1914.

Vakil, Kanaiyalal H. *At Ajanta.* Bombay, 1929.

Victoria and Albert Museum. *Indian Drawings: Wantage Collection.* London, 1932.

Welch, Stuart C. *Indian Painting 15th–19th Centuries from the Collection of Mrs. John F. Kennedy and J. K. Galbraith.* Harvard, 1965.

Yazdani, G. *Indian Art of the Buddhist Period.* Oxford, 1937.

Index

Index

203

treatment of women in painting, 103
peshwaz, 120
picture galleries (*chittra-sala*), 22
Pingal, Raja, 74
Plassey, Battle of, 13
poetry, 21, 106
Poongal, 74
portraits, 33, 106, 110, 111, 117, 122, 123, 126, 155, 168, 179
portraiture, *see* portraits
Pragjyotisha, 89
Prahlad, 82
Prakash Chand, Raja, 176, 177
Pratap, Rana, 157
Pritham Singh, 180
Prithipat Shah, 177
protruding eye, 100, 103, 154, 173
Punjab, 167, 173, 177, 178, 179, 182
Putana, 87

Radha, 9, 10, 39, 40, 86, 89, 90, 104, 166, 170
raga, 34–38, 103, 155
ragamala, see themes
ragini, 35–38, 103
Rai Singh, 161
Rajasthan, 35, 38, 75, 100, 128, 153, 165
Rajput princes, 75
Rajputs, 35
Rajput states, 162
Raj Singh, 165
Rama, 73, 83–86, 94, 128, 156
Ramayana, 75, 83–86, 126, 128, 156
Rambha, 81
Ram Dayal, artist, 183
Ranjha, artist, 179
Ranjit Dev, Raja, 179

Ranthambhar, 162
Rattan Singh, Rao, 162
Ravana, 83, 84, 85, 94
Ravi, river, 171, 182
Razmnamah, 78, 109
Rishabadeva, 94
rishis, 82
Ritusamhara, 40
Roe, Sir Thomas, 110
Rohini, 89
Romeo and Juliet, 74
Rousseau, Douanier, 164
Rudraka, 96
Rukh, Shah, 105, 106
Rukmini, 90
Ruknuddin, artist, 161
ruler, 25
Rupmati, 103

Saadi, poet, 102
sachchi tipai, 30
Saffavid dynasty, 106
sakti, 97
Sakuni, 77
Samarkand, 105
Sanga, Rana 157
Sangram Pal, Raja, 171
Sanju, artist, 183
sanni, 25
Sansar Chand, Raja, 174, 183
Sanwlah, artist, 109
Sarayu, river, 86
Saraswati, 81, 91
Sassanid empire, 105
Satrughna, 83
Satrusal, 162
Savant Singh, 165, 166
Sawai Jai Singh, 159
Schools of painting:
    Deccan, The, 15, 120–28
    Imperial Mughal, 23, 108–13
    Jain, 100–2
    Malwa, 102–3, 104, 172

    Mughal, 75, 78, 104–7, 124, 126–28, 162, 168
    Orissa, 103–4
    Oudh, 119–20
    Pahari, 15, 23, 38, 40, 74, 75, 78, 89, 92, 93, 122, 124, 158, 167–84
    Pala, 99
    Provincial Mughal, 117–19
    Rajput (Rajasthani), 15, 23, 38, 40, 78, 89, 92, 93, 114, 118, 122, 124, 128, 153–67
Shah Jahan, *see* Mughal emperors
Shahnamah, 109
Sham Das, artist, 177
shellac dye, 27, 28, 29
Shesha, 81, 94
Shiraz, 12, 102, 106
Shiva, god, 37, 38, 78, 79, 80, 81, 83, 84, 91, 92, 93, 95, 97
Shorapur, 124
Shree, 35, 36
Shuja-ud-Daula, Nawab, 119
Siddha, 95
Siddharta, 96
Sikhs, 35, 174, 180
Silparatna, 27
sindura tree, 29
Sita, 83, 84, 85, 86
Sivaji, 126
size, making of, 29
sky, depiction of, 14, 104, 124, 164, 166, 171, 178, 180
Somarupa, 22
Somnath, 93
Soni and Mahival, 75
South Indian schools, 125–26
Sri, *see* Lakshmi